DABBLER

KATHLEEN BLAVATT

A Subsidiary of
Henry Holt and Co., Inc.

First Edition—1995

Printed in the United States of America.

Library of Congress Cataloging-in-Publication Data

Blavatt, Kathleen.
    Dabbler / by Kathleen Blavatt.
       p.   cm
    ISBN 1-55828-449-4
    1. Computer graphics.   2. Dabbler.   I. Title
   T385.B577 1995
   006.6'869--dc20
                                                95-24986
                                                     CIP

10 9 8 7 6 5 4 3 2 1

MIS:Press books are available at special discounts for bulk purchases for sales promotions, premiums, fund-raising, or educational use. Special editions or book excerpts can also be created to specification.

For details contact: Special Sales Director
                          MIS:Press
                          a subsidiary of Henry Holt and Company, Inc.
                          115 West 18th Street
                          New York, New York 10011

Editor-in-Chief: Paul Farrell   **Managing & Development Editor:** Cary Sullivan

Tech Editor: Fractal Design   **Production Editor:** Stephanie Doyle

Copy Edit Manager: Shari Chappell   **Copy Editor:** Suzanne Ingrao

DEDICATION

Dabbler is dedicated to my husband Ray. Our mutual love for art and computers has brought us many wonderful experiences.

Many individuals presented artwork or assisted in the preparation of this book. I would like to express my appreciation and sincere thanks for all their help and support.

NOTE FOR WINDOWS USERS

Although *Dabbler* was written primarily for Macintosh users, please note that the interfaces for both the Windows and Macintosh versions of Fractal Design Corporation's Dabbler are similar enough that this book is a valuable reference tool for users on either platform.

PREFACE

I have a special affinity for the Fractal Design Corporation staff and its software. Its products opened my eyes to the ability to create fine art on computers. The first time I saw Painter software packaged in a gallon-size paint can, I knew it was special. Boy, was I right! When I tried the first version of Painter, all I could think was "WOW, this is wonderful, it's like doing real art!" I never looked at the computer in the same way again.

The first time I tried Fractal Painter I was reviewing it in conjunction with the Wacom pressure-sensitive drawing tablet for the San Diego Mac User Group. Shortly after the review was released, I received a call from Wacom, asking me to demonstrate for them at computer trade expositions. The first show I demonstrated at was Seybold in September 1992, which was when Wacom introduced the ArtZ tablet.

At Seybold, I met John Derry, an artist for Fractal Design Corporation. John and I spoke about Painter and its capabilities. I told John about my husband Ray and the work he does creating animation and art for interactive educational CDs for children. John wanted to hear our opinions of the Painter program and our preferred features. Soon after the show, we were on the phone with John. A few months later at MacWorld an upgrade of Painter was released, and to our delight some of the features we suggested were included.

My husband and I both demonstrated at that MacWorld. We met more of the Fractal Design Corporation staff there and have since formed a relationship with them. They use my art to demonstrate and promote their products.

I was excited when I first heard about Dabbler. It was innovative in that its interface was designed for beginning users and children, yet it still had many of the advanced features of Painter. When I first saw the art drawers, I felt this was a wonderful way to make art supplies easy to find and to provide a way to keep an art studio clean and organized. Another nice feature of Dabbler is that it takes up less RAM than Painter, so more people can use it.

In my experience teaching art to developmentally disabled adults, Dabbler and Painter have been wonderful tools. My students' familiarity with traditional art makes the transition to Dabbler quick with minimal instruction. Even deaf and physically disabled students find Dabbler easy to use.

As a professional illustrator, I have tried many drawing and paint programs, but I always come back to Fractal Design Corporation's software. No one makes a Pencil tool feel more like a real pencil. The company's Brush and Pen tools are wonderful. Liquids such as Distorto, and the many effects spark the user's imagination.

I think the best description of Dabbler I've heard came from Alex Pelayo, an eleven-year-old who submitted artwork for the *Dabbler* book. Alex said, "before I tried Dabbler I thought it was an okay program, but now that I've tried it, IT'S COOL!"

CONTENTS ▪ ▪ ▪ ▪ ▪ ▪ ▪ ▪ ▪

SECTION II: SESSIONS 81

THE SESSIONS

DABBLER ▪ ▪ ▪ ▪ ▪ ▪ ▪ ▪ ▪ ▪ ▪ ▪

SECTION I

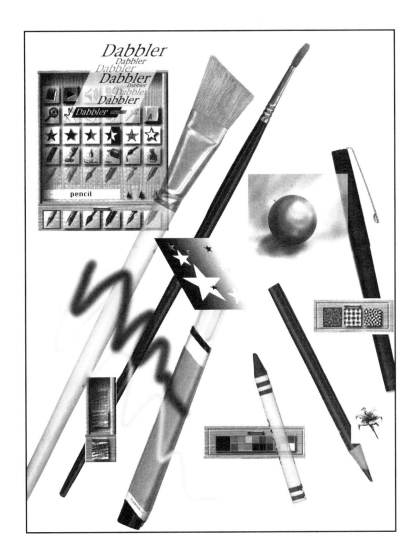

INTRODUCTION

COMPUTERS AND ART

Among the major advantages of creating art on the computer are that there's no mess or clean up, no toxic fumes, and a flexibility that can't be found with traditional mediums. Programs such as Dabbler allow artists to create artwork or manipulate scanned images that can be incorporated into current and future computer media technologies, taking full advantage of the computer as an art tool.

Beyond the current benefits of computers, the future promises to bring users spectacular technology. Technologies such as multimedia, edutainment, and virtual reality will become more and more a part of our lives, and programs like Dabbler give users the tools they need to feel at home with these technologies.

Why Dabbler Works for Beginning and Experienced Artists

Dabbler puts fun, creativity, and learning into one easy-to-use program. Intuitive menus and palettes, and emulation of a wide variety of natural media—from crayons and brushes to surface textures—make learning easy for both children and adults. Within minutes, first-time computer users are drawing.

Using Dabbler is like having an art studio at your fingertips. Its tools and features allow users to explore art, learn the fundamental elements of art, and incorporate their work into other media. In short, Fractal Design Corporation's Dabbler is changing the way people think about computers and art because it merges technology and traditional art more seamlessly than ever before.

Traditionally trained artists, as well as beginners, find Dabbler easy to use. Not only can art styles created with traditional media be reproduced in Dabbler, but the convenience of a computer will have many artists developing new styles. With advanced capabilities such as Stencils, Cloning, and Tracing, users will find a flexibility in working with Dabbler that can't be found with conventional media. For example, traditional mediums that will not mix (such as oils and watercolors) will mix in Dabbler.

Dabbler can be used with a pressure-sensitive computer drawing tablet and stylus (the pen that comes with the tablet). The benefits of pressure sensitivity include variation of line widths, opacity, and amount of medium applied. Pressure-sensitive tablets bring the user much closer to the look and feel of conventional art mediums, while allowing users to go beyond the limits of traditional mediums.

WHAT YOU'LL FIND IN THIS BOOK

In Section I, Dabbler will familiarize you with the program's tools, brushes, effects, palettes, and general operation of the program. Next, advanced methods of working with Dabbler will be introduced, which will allow you to further develop and hone your skills. Supplemental art, as well as hints and tips, are included throughout the book.

Section II consists of drawing sessions that incorporate material covered in Section I. These sessions are step-by-step projects that will teach you how to use Dabbler's features, functions, and tools into finished art. The sessions also cover a variety of techniques and principles of art. Issues such as composition, styles, forming subjects with lines and shapes, and figure and portrait drawing are included.

Many of the sessions can be done with traditional tools. I strongly suggest doing them both on the computer and with traditional art supplies whenever possible, since it's important for users to see and feel how real mediums work. For example, chalk picks up paper texture while spray paint does not. Knowing this, the Dabbler artists can select the appropriate mediums for a natural (or unnatural!) effect. In other words, Dabbler emulates mediums so well that it greatly benefits artists to have traditional knowledge and experience.

Since a good artist should be familiar with a variety of art styles, Section II also includes a variety of computer artists' work and descriptions of how each piece was created. The artwork was created by professional artists, children, autistic savants, and developmentally disabled adults.

Now you're ready to embark on a creative adventure into the realm of computer art…

SETUP AND INSTALLATION

INSTALLING DABBLER FOR THE MACINTOSH

Macintosh system requirements:

- Macintosh or Power Macintosh models (except Plus, SE, Classic and Powerbook 100).

- Hard disk with 8 megabytes of RAM and 10 MB hard disk space.

- Apple system software 7.0 or later.

- CD-ROM drive.

- Color or grayscale monitor.

Window system requirements:

▪ 486 DX or Pentium IBM PC or compatible with 8 MB of RAM.

▪ Microsoft Windows 3.1 or later, including Windows 95 (card required for sound).

▪ Hard disk.

▪ Color monitor.

▪ Super VGA (256 colors), 16-bit or 24-bit graphics card.

▪ CD-ROM drive.

Dabbler supports various pressure-sensitive tablets such as Wacom, Calcomp, Summa Graphics, Hitachi, and Kurta.

You must disable virus protection software before installing Dabbler or the program may not install properly.

Installing from CD for the Macintosh

The Dabbler CD contains the Dabbler 2 Application, Brushes, Interface, Dabbler On-line Manual, Sessions, Sounds, Settings, Sketchpad, Stencils, (over 3,000 stencils) Stencils folder, Templates, Textures, Textures folder, Tools icons, Fonts folder, Quickview, Stock Photo folder (100 photo images), Walter Foster Animations, and Walter Foster Cartoons.

1   Insert the Dabbler CD into your CD drive. Click and read the **Read Me** file before starting installation. This file provides important information such as software, hardware, or product conflicts, extra notes, and a general overview of installation procedures.

2   Double-click on the **Dabbler Installer** icon.

3 Select the hard drive and folder for Dabbler.

4 Click **Install**.

Launching Dabbler for the Macintosh

To launch Dabbler 2 for the Macintosh, do the following:

1 Open by double-clicking on the **Dabbler** icon.

2 A dialog box appears asking you to enter your name and your Dabbler serial number. The serial number is found on your registration card. Once you've entered your name and serial number, click **OK**.

3 Electronic registration in Dabbler 2 will allow users with a modem to transmit their registration information directly to Fractal Design. When you boot-up Dabbler 2 for the first time, you will get the normal Dabbler serialization dialog box. After you fill out that dialog successfully, you will get a registration dialog box that contains information similar to our registration card. You will have the option of filling it out and registering, or postponing registration. If you register, the software will look for a modem on your system, and if successful, will dial-out and download the the registration information on-site at Fractal. If not successful, you have the option of printing the registration information out and faxing, or mailing it to Fractal (using the Fractal business-reply envelope). If the user does not have a printer, they can fill out the registration card and mail it to Fractal Design.

If you decide to postpone registration you will get the same registration screen the next time you start the program and for two more times afterward. If you have not registered after seeing the registration screen for 4 times, the program will offer you the option of declining to register.

The registration information is stored in a special file in the application's directory which is scanned at startup. If this file is not present (the program was reinstalled, or copied to a different machine without this file), you will be prompted to register again.

4   Another dialog box appears asking you to select a third-party, Photoshop-compatible plug-in. Select a plug-in from your hard drive, and double-click on it. This lets Dabbler know which folders or directories contain the plug-ins, allowing you to access and use their special effects and drivers from within Dabbler. To bring up this dialog box in the future, press the **Command** key while double-clicking on the **Dabbler** icon.

Be sure to fill out the registration card and send it to Fractal Design Corporation.

BASIC DABBLER

This chapter covers the following topics:

- Drawer Menus
  - Extras Drawer
  - Tools Drawer
    - Tool Sizes
    - Drawing and Painting Tools
    - Stencil Tools
    - Special Tools

- Color Drawer
  - Color Relationships and Terminology
- Papers Drawer
  - Stroke Textures
- Clone, Tracing Paper, and Page Selection Drawer
  - Cloning
  - Tracing Paper
  - Page Selection
- Dabbler's Menus
  - File Menu
  - Edit Menu
  - Effects Menu
  - Options Menu
  - Tutors Menu

Dabbler is easy to use and understand because the interface is set up like a traditional art studio and the icons are easy to recognize. The program provides wonderful tools, a simple interface, and Tutor Sessions that inspire creativity.

Many of the tools in Dabbler emulate traditional mediums that allow you to draw in your own style and to imitate other styles. Dabbler also takes you beyond patterning your art after natural mediums. Mediums that would not work together in real life do in Dabbler. For example, water can be mixed with oil paint. Section II and the Gallery include many samples of the vast array of art that can be created with Dabbler's tools.

This section will cover the basics of Dabbler, including its tools, interface, menus, and options. Keyboard commands and helpful suggestions are also provided. You will be introduced to Dabbler's tools and functions, which encourage creativity and experimentation.

DRAWER MENUS

The first items you see when you open Dabbler are the drawers. The drawers hold the Extras, Tools, Colors, Textures, and the Clone/Tracing Paper/Page Selection. To open and close the drawers, simply click on the handle located on the front of the drawer.

FIGURE 3.1 **DABBLER'S DRAWERS**

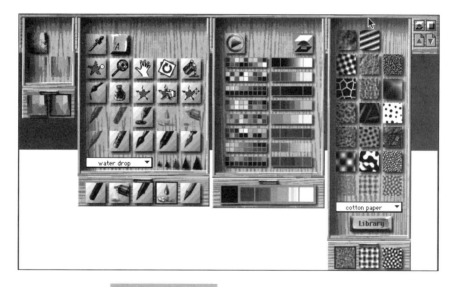

FIGURE 3.2 **OPEN DRAWERS**

Extras Drawer

The first drawer on the left is the Extras drawer, which contains variations for some tools. Once a tool is selected, a characteristics icon will appear on the face of the Extras drawer.

FIGURE 3.3   EXTRAS DRAWER

Some tools may have more than two choices appearing on the face of the drawer. To access other selections, click on the Extras drawer to open it. Click on your choice, and it will appear on the face of the Extras drawer. A red box will appear around your selection to show that it is active.

FIGURE 3.4   OPEN EXTRAS DRAWER,
WATER TOOL SELECTIONS

Drawing and Painting tool choices will include different opacities of strokes, stroke styles, and bleeds.

The following section includes information about the tool characteristics available in the Extras drawer, as well as a description of the items found in the Tools drawer.

Tools Drawer

The Tools drawer holds many items. These include Tool Tip Sizes, Drawing and Painting Tools, Stencil Tools, and Special Tools. A helpful feature of the Tools drawer is that it includes a window that displays the name of the selected tool.

FIGURE 3.5   **THE TOOLS DRAWER WINDOW**
WITH THE PENCIL TOOL SELECTED

When a tool is selected from the inside of the Tools drawer, it will replace the tool that appears on the face of the Tools drawer. A red outline indicates which tool is selected.

TOOL SIZES

Five triangles are displayed in the front right corner of the Tools drawer. These triangles represent Tool Size Tips, ranging from small to large. The selected size is displayed in red.

FIGURE 3.6   **THE TOOL SIZE TIPS**

You can also use the keyboard command Tab to change the tip size of your tool. If you use the Tab key with the Spacebar, you can make incremental size changes.

N O T E

Different brushes and drawing tools have different stroke characteristics, depending on the tip size selected. When selecting a tip size, it's important to remember that certain art mediums lend themselves to transparent or opaque styles, while some tools will pick up texture better than others.

DRAWING AND PAINTING TOOLS

What makes Dabbler superior to many paint programs is its ability to make the Drawing and Painting tools look and feel like traditional art tools. Having pressure-sensitive capabilities (when used with a pressure-sensitive drawing tablet) adds to Dabbler's ability to emulate real mediums.

FIGURE 3.7   **DABBLER'S DRAWING AND PAINTING TOOLS**

The first and second rows toward the front of the Tools drawer hold Drawing and Painting tools. Following are descriptions of these tools.

 ## PENCIL TOOL

The Pencil tool gives you a choice of a **2B** or **colored** pencil in the Extras drawer. This tool is commonly used to create a base layout for many illustrations, just as traditional artists will often use a pencil to create their basic sketches.

FIGURE 3.8 **DABBLER'S PENCIL TOOL EMULATES A REAL PENCIL**

 ## ERASER TOOL

The Eraser tool works like a real eraser. Dabbler offers two choices for the Eraser tool on the Extras drawer: **Eraser** produces a soft, transparent erase (depending on the stroke and pressure used); **Flat Erase** produces a solid, hard-edged rub that goes straight through to the surface. The Eraser tool will erase any Dabbler or plug-in mediums.

FIGURE 3.9   ERASE AND FLAT ERASE COMBINATION

 Beyond erasing, the Eraser tool is very useful for creating highlights and reflections.

 ## BRUSH TOOL

The Brush tool is used for creating solid, opaque strokes. Using the Brush tool with the large tip allows you to paint over large areas. The Brush tool's strokes will pick up texture around the stroke's edges.

FIGURE 3.10   A VARIETY OF BRUSH TOOL TIP SIZES WERE USED TO CREATE THE FLOWER SAMPLE

CRAYON TOOL

The Crayon tool simulates the waxy feel of real crayons. This medium picks up texture well.

Layering different color Crayon tool strokes creates interesting color blends.

FIGURE 3.11   **CRAYON SAMPLE**

 ## PEN TOOL

The Pen tool creates ink lines. From the Extras drawer, you have a choice of Transparent or Opaque inks. The Transparent selection picks up some texture. Opaque is a solid line that does *not* pick up texture. A woodcut effect is achieved with a black background (which can be applied with a fill), the Pen tool with white selected, and Opaque turned on in the Extras drawer.

 **The Pen tool provides solid color, which is useful for creating outlines and emphasis. With white selected as your color, the Pen tool produces a solid line when drawing over black and dark colors.**

FIGURE 3.12   STROKE AND CROSS-HATCHING TECHNIQUES

FIGURE 3.13   WOODCUT STYLE CREATED WITH THE WHITE
PEN TOOL ON A BLACK BACKGROUND

 ## MARKER TOOL

As with other tools, the Marker tool will produce a variety of results according to the tip size you select. For example, the small tip emulates a fine point, and the two largest tips emulate felt pen markers. The Marker colors bleed when mixed with other Marker strokes (just like a real marker!).

FIGURE 3.14 **THE MARKER TOOL WAS USED TO CREATE THIS FACE**

 CHALK TOOL

The Chalk tool emulates chalk wonderfully. It picks up texture well and can be smudged with the Water Drop tool to create a softer look.

FIGURE 3.15 **HOW THE CHALK TOOL PICKS UP PAPER TEXTURES**

Some pressure-sensitive tablets on the market have a tilt feature. This lets you angle the stylus, allowing you to draw more like a professional chalk artist, using the thumb underneath and the four fingers on top to hold the stylus.

 ## OIL PAINT TOOL

The Oil Paint tool lets you apply paint in the **Impressionistic** or **Seurat** styles (you can choose the style from the Extras drawer). This tool works well when you're building up layers of color strokes or using Auto Clone.

FIGURE 3.16 **DOLPHIN CREATED WITH SEURAT SELECTION**

 ## WATER DROP TOOL

The Water Drop tool is effective for blending, smudging, and softening colors. The Extras drawer offers several choices of water that include **Frosty Water**, **Regular Water**, and **Grainy Water**. The Water tool will work on any previously applied mediums.

FIGURE 3.17   **SOFT BLENDING ACHIEVED WITH THE WATER DROP TOOL**

 SPRAY PAINT TOOL

The Spray Paint tool puts out a soft, smooth stroke that achieves an airbrush effect. Light strokes are transparent. As strokes are layered or pressure is increased, they become opaque. This tool works well for retouching photo images.

FIGURE 3.18   **THE SPRAY PAINT TOOL CREATES SOFT, SUBTLE BLENDING**

LIQUID BRUSH TOOL

The Liquid Brush tool adds "liquid" to your palette. It emulates a fluid and mixes with previously applied mediums so that strokes can be pulled and swirled through your artwork. The Liquid Brush tool creates melting, marbling, and distortion effects.

FIGURE 3.19 **A DISTORTION EFFECT CREATED WITH THE LIQUID BRUSH TOOL**

 ## INK BOTTLE TOOL

By applying a tip size, the Ink Bottle tool gives you five styles of ink lines and dots to choose from: The small tip produces a single pixel fine line; the small medium tip creates pixel dust, which gives a stippling effect; medium tip produces random dots to produce a leaky pen effect; large medium tip makes a random drop; Large tip makes a very large random dot.

A scratchboard effect is achieved with a black background (which can be applied with a fill), using the Pen tool with white selected.

FIGURE 3.20   FINE LINE, PIXEL DUST, AND LEAKY PEN

FIGURE 3.21   FINE LINE SCRATCHBOARD TECHNIQUE

 The Ink Bottle brush with the medium-size tip selected provides a nice stippling effect, which works well for creating flower centers, details in sand, and details on animals (such as a cat's nose).

FIGURE 3.22	CAT FACE WITH PIXEL DUST STIPPLING DETAILS CREATED WITH THE INK BOTTLE TOOL

STENCIL TOOLS

The Stencil tools are symbolized by a variety of star icons displayed in the Tools drawer. The Stencil, Polygonal, and Freehand tools allow you to block out areas so that you can draw or fill on either the outside or inside of the stencil you create. These tools work with the Paint Bucket, Effects, or any of the Drawing and Painting tools. You can use the **Delete** button to delete contents in or around the stencil.

When the Stencil, Polygonal, and Freehand tools display a white background and the star is filled with green, it means you can fill the inside of your stencil shape. To temporarily mask out your stencil in order to fill in the background, click on the **Stencil** tool. The Stencil tool will then show the star symbol reversed out to white with green strokes around it.

 ### STENCIL

When the **Stencil** tool is selected, the Extras drawer is full of stencil choices that include **Square**, **Circle**, **Star**, and **Heart**.

FIGURE 3.23   **DEFAULT STENCILS IN EXTRAS DRAWER**

There is also a **Library** selection in the Extras drawer. By clicking on **Library** you can bring in other stencil **Libraries** selections.

The **Libraries** are full of many shapes, symbols, and maps. These stencils can be incorporated into a variety of both fine art and graphics projects.

FIGURE 3.24   **A STENCIL LIBRARY SELECTION IN THE EXTRAS DRAWER**

FIGURE 3.25   **FILLED STENCIL FIGURES FROM THE STENCIL LIBRARY**

 To constrain shapes proportionally, hold down the **Shift** key.

 FLOAT

The image inside a stenciled area can be moved and repositioned by using the Float tool.

The image can be copied by selecting it and pressing the **Option** key. Positioning changes can be made while the stencil is selected, but once deselected, it becomes part of the image.

 POLYGONAL

The Polygonal stencil allows you to draw shapes with straight lines.

Press the **Enter** key to automatically close a shape at its origin points.

FIGURE 3.26   **THE TEAPOT WAS CREATED WITH THE POLYGONAL STENCIL TOOL AND BUCKET FILLS**

 To constrain lines to 90°or 45° angles, hold down the **Shift** key.

 ## FREEHAND

The Freehand stencil allows you to draw freeform shapes. It is a great time-saving device for creating solid shapes. This tool works well for cropping, deleting, or filling backgrounds.

SPECIAL TOOLS

The Tools drawer contains the Special tools that will help you work faster and more precisely. The following section describes each of the Special tools.

FIGURE 3.27   THE FLOWERS WERE CREATED WITH THE
FREEHAND STENCIL TOOL AND BUCKET FILLS

 MAGNIFIER

The Magnifier tool allows you to enlarge images simply by clicking on them. It will zoom in on selected portions of your image, allowing you to see more intricate details and draw more precisely. You can also zoom out from an image by clicking on the **Magnifier** tool a second time (a minus sign will appear in the Magnifier tool). To get back into enlargement mode, either click on the **Magnifier** tool again or press the Command key.

 Dabbler's zoom capacity ranges from **8.3%** to **1200%**. The Option menu allows you to change these percentages by choosing the **Zoom Factor** command. Key commands are: (Macintosh) **Command-Spacebar: Zoom In command-spacebar option: Zoom Out.** (Windows) **Ctrl-Spacebar: Zoom In. Shift-Ctrl-Spacebar: Zoom out**

N O T E

 GRABBER

The Grabber tool allows you to move and reposition the whole image area. If you hold down the **Spacebar**, the Grabber tool will automatically appear. The Grabber tool will also let you recenter your image by clicking on it once. To enable this function, the image size must be **100%**.

PAGE ROTATE

The Page Rotate tool lets you turn your image area up to 360°, allowing you to work at a more comfortable drawing angle. Click on the **Page Rotate** tool, and then click in the image window. A square with an arrow inside appears in the image area. The square and arrow determine your rotation angle (hold down the **Shift** key to rotate the page by 90° increments). Release the mouse button when the page is angled to your liking.

To access the Page Rotation tool from the keyboard, press the **Control** key while clicking and dragging the image to get the desired angle. The **Control** key will also bring the image back to normal orientation by clicking on it when the Page Rotate tool is *not* selected.

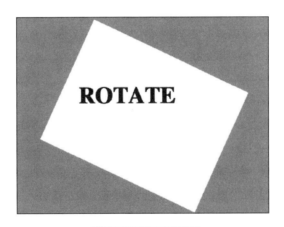

FIGURE 3.28

 PAINT BUCKET

The Paint Bucket tool is a great time-saving device. It is used to fill backgrounds, closed shapes, and stencils. Solid or graduated color fills are applied by making a color palette choice, selecting the **Paint Bucket** tool, and clicking inside or outside your shape (if selected, a line will also change color).

If there is no stencil present, the Paint Bucket will fill entire image or contiguous pixels of the same color. The keyboard command to fill backgrounds, shapes, and stencils is **Command-F**. The keyboard command will produce a fill with the currently selected color.

 ## DROPPER TOOL

The Dropper tool is used to sample colors. By clicking on a color in the image with the Dropper tool, you replace the selected color in the palette, and it becomes part of the current color palette and can be used in the future. By using this technique you can create a custom palette that matches previously used colors from your image.

The keyboard command to access the Dropper tool is the **Option** key.

 ## TEXT TOOL

The Text tool is represented by a capital 'A' on a keyboard button. The cursor changes to a flashing text cursor. Click on the image to set the origin point for your text. The Text tool works in conjunction with the Type Styles found under **Option** in the menu (or double-click on the **Text** tool icon to bring up the Type Styles option box). Type Styles allows you to choose fonts/dingbats and sizes.

FIGURE 3.29   **THE SHADOW WAS CREATED WITH THE SOFTEN EFFECT**

COLOR

Color Principles and Terminology

Before moving to a discussion of Dabbler's color capabilities, it's important to understand some basic color principles and terminology.

PRIMARY, SECONDARY, AND INTERMEDIATE COLORS

Red, blue, and yellow are called *primary colors*. All other colors are a result of mixing primary colors, while black is the absence of color, and white is the inclusion of all colors.

Secondary colors are the result of mixing primary colors. For example, red + yellow = orange, yellow + blue = green, and red + blue = violet.

Intermediate colors are the result of mixing one primary color with one secondary color. These colors are yellow-orange, red-orange, red-purple, blue-purple, blue-green, and yellow-green.

BASIC COLOR TERMS

Hue	The name for a pure color.
Tint	A color with white added to it.
Shade	A color with black added to it.
Tone	A color with gray added to it.
Intensity	The brightness or dullness of a color.
Value	The lightness or darkness of a color.

Color sets the mood of a piece. *Pastel* colors are made from a color mixed with white. Pastels such as pink, peach, light yellow, and light green are considered pleasant, friendly colors. *Cool* colors are the darker hues on the color wheel. These include blue, purple, violet, and green. *Cool colors* are somber colors. *Warm* colors are the bright hues on the color wheel. These colors include red, orange, and yellow. Warm colors tend to excite the viewer and grab attention. Most artwork has a mix of colors and the presence of black and/or white, but the dominant color tends to set the mood.

Color schemes, usage, and examples are covered in the Sessions in Section II and in the Gallery.

Color Drawer

When you first install Dabbler and open the Color drawer, Dabbler offers a selection of premade solid color palettes that include bright colors, earth tones, colors and their tints, flesh tones, greens and blues, etc. In addition, there are graduated palettes. You can customize the colors in both the solid and graduated palettes by using Dabbler's Color Wheel.

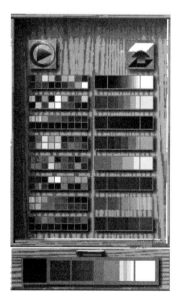

FIGURE 3.30   **THE COLOR DRAWER**

FIGURE 3.31   **THE COLOR WHEEL**

At the top of the Color drawer is a Color Wheel icon. Double-click on the **Color Wheel** icon and it will fill the drawer. You may also access the Color Wheel from the front of the drawer by double-clicking on the large color square to the left of the palettes.

The outside ring of the Color Wheel allows you to select colors, and the triangle on the inside of the Color Wheel lets you choose tints and shades of the selected color. When you select a color from the outside ring, the color of the inside triangle changes simultaneously.

Different values of a color are selected from the inside triangle of the Color Wheel. The closer you move your selection toward white, the lighter the color will be. If you move toward black, the color will become darker. The closer your selection is to the right tip of the triangle, the purer the color will be. To select white or black, go to the furthest tip of white or black on the triangle.

The color you've specified with the Color Wheel will appear in the large square of the palette that appears on the face of the drawer. If you want to save the color for future use, select one of the small squares in the palette and then choose the color you want from the Color drawer. If you only need the color once and don't want to change your palette, select the large square on your palette.

FIGURE 3.32   **THE SOLID COLOR PALETTE**

FIGURE 3.33   **THE GRADUATED COLOR PALETTE**

Changes to the graduated palette are made by clicking on the squares at the ends of the graduation bar and selecting a new color, or clicking anywhere within the graduation bar and selecting a color.

At the bottom of the Color drawer are faded **solid palette** and **graduated palette** icons. These icons allow you to change the style of your current palette from solid to graduated and vice versa.

FIGURE 3.34   **PALETTE STYLE ICONS**

For some projects, you may want to set up custom color palettes ahead of time. This will allow you to work more efficiently and ensure that your colors are consistent.

Papers Drawer

The ability to choose paper textures is one of Dabbler's finest features, providing a tremendous amount of versatility. Many effects can be achieved by applying texture. Textures add interest, detail, and realism, as well as creating the appearance of different canvases and surfaces.

FIGURE 3.35   **DABBLER'S PAPER TEXTURES**

Three textures are visible on the front of the Papers drawer. To access more textures, click on the **Papers drawer** handle, select a texture, and it will appear on the front of the Papers drawer. A pop-up menu shows the selected texture's name.

Each texture can be inverted (reversing the texture's dark and light areas) by clicking once on its icon.

Dabbler gives you access to other paper textures. Click on Library in the Texture drawer. A folder in Dabbler will come up giving you a selection of other libraries to choose from. Open the library of your choice. It will replace the current library in the Papers drawer.

Dabbler's CD supplies more than 120 new texture palettes in the libraries. Dabbler also supports any Fractal Painter libraries or *Sensational Surface* libraries by ArtBeat.

FIGURE 3.36   **A NEW DABBLER LIBRARY**

STROKE TEXTURES

The textures in the Paper drawer work with the Pencil, Chalk, Crayon, Transparent Pen, Grainy, and Frosty Water tools. The ease with which textures can be mixed allows artists to use Dabbler's capabilities to go beyond what could be achieved with natural mediums.

FIGURE 3.37

 With Dabbler's texture selection you can easily create the look of baskets, fur, sand, water, leaves, scales, and other surfaces that would require much more time and effort to create with traditional artists' tools and mediums.

Cloning, Tracing Paper, and Page Section Drawer

 ## CLONING

Dabbler's Cloning feature is an artist's dream come true. It makes a copy of an original image, allowing experimentation without changing the original artwork.

FIGURE 3.38

The **Cloning** icon is located on the drawer to the far right. When the **Cloning** icon is selected, a larger copy of it will appear on the front of the Color Palette drawer to show that it's in use. Your current image will then be a clone.

You can paint over the cloned image by using any of Dabbler's Drawing and Painting tools with any textures. You can also change your tools and textures as you work.

FIGURE 3.39A **THIS SCANNED PHOTO WAS CLONED USING THE CHALK AND SPRAY PAINT TOOLS**

FIGURE 3.39B **CLONED IMAGE USING THE CHALK AND OIL PAINT TOOLS WITH IMPRESSIONISTIC SELECTED FROM THE EXTRAS DRAWER**

Auto Clone

You can automatically clone your image by selecting a Drawing or Painting tool, then selecting the **Auto Clone** command from the Effects menu.

FIGURE 3.40A   SCANNED PHOTO OF A LAKE SCENE

FIGURE 3.40B   CLONED IMAGE USING THE SEURAT TOOL

TRACING PAPER

One of the most helpful features of Dabbler is the Tracing Paper utility. The Tracing Paper feature lets you trace over your original artwork or scan, and lets you clean up or redraw an image. This ability can save you a great deal of time.

The Tracing Paper function is accessed through an icon that appears on the far right drawer. The Tracing icon lets you turn a page into tracing paper, which means that the image on the previous page will be visible through the page. To have a blank piece of tracing paper you need to add a new page. (If you turn a page with a image on it into tracing paper you will have that image and the tracing combined.) Click on the Tracing icon, and your paper will become semi-transparent with your underlying image appearing through the tracing paper. Now you can trace the image.

When you've finished tracing, click the **Tracing** icon and your drawing will become opaque. This image is automatically saved in the Sketchpad.

 ## PAGE SELECTION

The two triangles below the **Cloning** and **Tracing** icons are for scrolling backward and forward to other pages in your Sketchpad.

DABBLER'S MENUS
File Menu

New Sketchpad   A dialog box will appear when you click on **New Sketchpad**. This dialog box lets you create and customize a new Sketchpad. **Width, Height, Resolution, Number of Pages,** and **Paper Color** specifications can all be set in this dialog box. (Refer to Chapter 4 for more information about setting Sketchpad size, resolution, and paper color.)

New Flipbook   Adds a new Flipbook that can be saved in your Dabbler folder. A Flipbook Setup dialog box will appear when you click on **New Flipbook**. The dialog box lets you customize settings for your new Flipbook. **Size, Number of Frames, Binding,** and **layout** specifications can all be set in this dialog box. (Refer to Chapter 4 for more information.)

```
┌─────────────────────────────────────────────┐
│  File   Edit   Effects   Options   Tutors    │
└─────────────────────────────────────────────┘
```

FIGURE 3.41

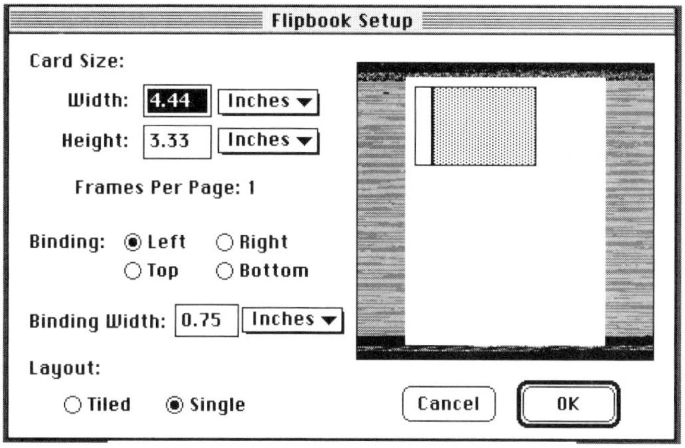

Flipbook Setup

Card Size:

Width: **4.44** | Inches ▾

Height: 3.33 | Inches ▾

Frames Per Page: 1

Binding: ● Left   ○ Right
         ○ Top   ○ Bottom

Binding Width: 0.75 | Inches ▾

Layout:
○ Tiled   ● Single

Cancel   OK

FIGURE 3.42

Open (Command-O) Opens an existing file or scanned photograph. The file is added to the current Sketchpad.

Import Image Imports a file from another program.

Save Page As... **(Command-S)** Allows you to name and save a file independent of a Sketchpad. A dialog box lets you select the folder/directory where the file is to be placed. A type box lets you name your file. Another box lets you uncompress your file if you wish. The type box allows you to select a file format. Dabbler file formats include RIFF, TIFF, PICT, Photoshop, BMP, TARGA, and JPEG (RIFF is Dabblers default format). When all the selections are specified, click on Save. For more information about formats, look under Browse Pages, Folder.

Revert Page Returns a file to its last saved state, including Sketchpad pages.

Acquire Allows you to scan from within Dabbler or to acquire software from other input devices. Scanner interface software must be Photoshop-compatible.

Export Exports a file to various output devices, such as film recorders or tape backup systems, using a Photoshop export module.

TWAIN Acquire... (Windows only) Allows you to scan from within Dabbler using TWAIN.

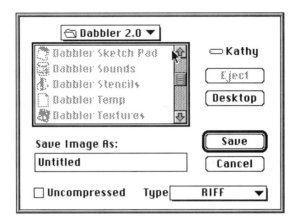

FIGURE 3.43

N O T E

TWAIN is a general method for acquiring any raster image and is supported by several software programs and scanner manufacturers. To access your scanner, you must first tell Dabbler which scanner you'll be using. Choose the **Select TWAIN Source...** command from the File menu. A dialog box appears allowing you to select any scanner with a TWAIN driver that's available on your computer. Select a scanner, then select the **TWAIN Acquire...** command, which brings up your scanner's software interface. In order for TWAIN to work, you must have the TWAIN source manager—a file called **TWAIN.DLL**—in your Windows system directory. **TWAIN.DLL** comes with scanners that support TWAIN. If your scanner doesn't include **TWAIN.DLL**, ask your scanner manufacturer how you can get a copy. Fractal Design Corporation cannot supply you with **TWAIN.DLL**. If **TWAIN.DLL** is not in your Windows system directory, the **Acquire** and **Select Source** menu items will be gray (in other words, inaccessible).

TWAIN Source...	(Windows only) see TWAIN Acquire....
Page Setup...	(Macintosh only) Establishes parameters for printing a Dabbler document. The Black and White option must be selected when printing on a black-and-white printer, or a PostScript error will occur when the document is printing.

Print Setup...	(Windows only) Establishes parameters for printing a Dabbler document.
Print...	Prints the open Dabbler file.
Quit (Command-Q)	(Macintosh only) Closes the Dabbler application.
Exit	(Windows only) Closes the Dabbler application.

Edit Menu

Undo (Command-Z)	Undoes the last performed operation.
Cut (Command-X)	Removes a selected area from the image window and places it on the Clipboard.
Copy (Command C)	Copies a selected area from the image window and places it on the Clipboard (the original selection remains in the image window).
Paste (Command-V)	Places the contents of the Clipboard in the image window.
Clear	Removes a selected area from the image window, permanently deleting it.
Add Page (Command-N)	Adds a new piece of paper to the current Sketchpad.
Delete Page	A dialog box lets you specify the pages to be deleted.
Browse Pages	The Tools drawer window will display **Sketchpad, Pushpin, Folder,** and **Trash Can** icons.
	The Sketchpad is much like a real sketchpad in that you can save your work in it, turn to a new sheet of paper or back to a previously drawn sketch, and throw unwanted artwork into the trash.
	Clicking on the bottom sheet of the Sketchpad turns pages forward and brings up new, clean pages. Click on the top page of the Sketchpad to go backward. The final page selected will be the one displayed in the image area.

PAPER STACK

A new page can be added by grabbing a piece of paper from the Paper Stack icon and dragging it to the Sketchpad. A Sketchpad can hold a total of 99 pages, but it's a good idea to keep it shorter than that so as little computer space as possible is used.

FIGURE 3.44

TRASH CAN

Throw away artwork by dragging the selected page into the **Trash Can** icon. If you want to retrieve a discarded image, click on the **Crumpled Paper** icon in the **Trash Can**, and drag it back onto the Sketchpad. (Remember, each page in the Sketchpad adds to the memory size of the Sketchpad.)

 **By periodically cleaning out old, unwanted images, you can decrease the size of your Sketchpad.**

FOLDER

The Folder utility allows you to save images independently from the Sketchpad. To do this, drag your image from the Sketchpad to the Folder. A dialog box for naming your file will appear with a pop-up menu for specifying file type. Enter the name of your image and select a file type.

File formats include:

RIFF	(Raster Image File Format) This is Dabbler's default file format. This format makes the file size smaller than other format selections. It's important to keep the Uncompressed Option in the Set Preferences dialog box turned OFF when saving in RIFF format.
TIFF	(Tagged Image File Format) This a common format used to exchange documents between applications. IBM-compatible and Next systems support TIFF.
PICT	A commonly used Macintosh format. Macintosh's clipboard uses the PICT format.
PHOTOSHOP	The native 24-bit format of Photoshop. Once a file is opened in Photoshop it can be changed from RGB (screen colors) to CMYK (process colors), which is a necessary step for process printing.
BMP	(Bitmap Files) This is the main format used by Microsoft Windows' Clipboard.
Targa	Used by high-end, PC-based computers. You can choose the resolution of the files.
EPS	(Encapsulated PostScript) Used for desktop separation. EPS files cannot be reopened in Dabbler, so it's important to keep a backup in a different format if you wish to reopen the artwork.

The Folder also allows you to access other files, such as scanned images. To retrieve a file, click on the Folder, select the file from the File menu and click on **Open**.

If your document size is different from your Sketchpad size, a dialog box appears. You can select either enlarge to fit or crop to fit.

You may want to save this file with a different name in order to leave the original file intact. Choose **Save As** from the File menu, type a new name in the dialog box, and click **Save**.

Pushpin

Use the Pushpin utility to reorder the pages in the Sketchpad. Drag the selected page to the **Pushpin** icon. Click the desired location in the Sketchpad, and drag it over from the **Pushpin** icon to the Sketchpad.

Sketchpads can grow in memory size so you may want to store full Sketchpads on backup disks to allow room for new ones. For more information about creating new Sketchpads, refer to Chapter 4.

Go To Page	A dialog box appears for you to type in the desired page you want to go to. Once the page number is typed, select **OK**. You also have the option of canceling.
Select All (Command-A)	Selects the entire image.
Deselect (Command-D)	Deselects what is currently selected.
Reselect (Command-R)	Reselects stenciled areas that have been deselected.
Set Preferences...	Sets certain aspects of how Dabbler will work. For example, the color of your cursor and the direction it faces can be changed from this menu selection. The mouse control lets you adjust mouse pressure with a slidebar. The **Temp File Volume** can be changed from the Set Preferences... dialog box (this is the disk to which Dabbler will write a temporary file based on the size of the file you have opened—a duplicate of this file is stored in the temp file at the original size while the file is opened—this temporary file is used by Dabbler for several of its operations, including **Undo** and **Fade**). If you have more than one volume, you can choose the disk you wish to use as the **Temp File Volume** in the pop-up menu.

Sketchpad **JPEG** compression is another option in the dialog box. **JPEG** discards extra data, so once it has been compressed and then uncompressed, it will not be identical to the original, though in most cases it's indistinguishable. Do not use JPEG compression while in RIFF format because it's already compressed. The **plug-ins** selection brings up a dialog box that lets you select third-party plug-ins from your plug-in folder. Once the plug-ins are selected, you must restart your computer to activate them.

Sound Control gives you the option of changing or turning off the volume of Dabbler sounds. Selecting the left drawer icon turns off drawer sounds, and selecting the right drawer icon will turn on drawer sounds. Beneath the drawer icons are two pencil icons that symbolize tool sounds. The left pencil icon turns off tool sounds and the right pencil icon turns on tool sounds. The slider bar icon adjusts volume; sliding upward increases the volume and sliding downward decreases volume.

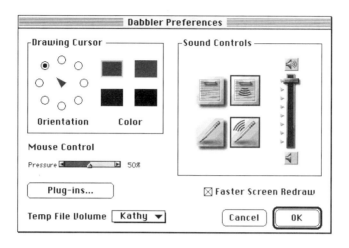

DABBLER'S SOUND UTILITY

For Windows Only: In the Windows Set Preferences dialog box, there is a button called **Window Setup.** Clicking this button displays memory and printing options.

N O T E

Effects Menu

Fill	Fills the stenciled or whole image area with your selected color.
Auto Clone	Automatically clones image with the selected Draw or Paint tool and Paper Texture.

The slider bar is included in several of the Effects dialog boxes. This feature gives you more control of the Effects by letting you adjust the amount of the effect applied.

SLIDER BAR

Fade

The Fade command reduces the application of the last effect. For example, if you perform a fill, the fade command will reduce the opacity. If you perform a Texturize, the Fade command will soften the effect. A dialog box will show how your faded image will appear. A slider bar lets you adjust the amount of Fade from 0% to 100%.

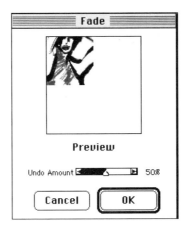

FIGURE 3.47

The Fade effect lets you make your images transparent. With this effect, you can layer see-through objects over one another, creating a layered, transparent image.

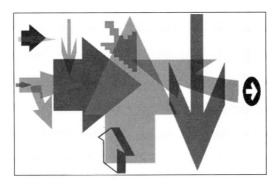

FIGURE 3.48   FADE EFFECTS ON LAYERED IMAGES

Glass Distortion

This effect makes artwork appear as if it is being seen through glass with the selected texture characteristics. When you select **Glass Distortion**, a dialog box will show you what your image will look like. A slider bar lets you adjust the amount of distortion. Glass Distortion can be applied over the whole image or a selected area defined by the Polygonal, Freehand, or Stencil tools.

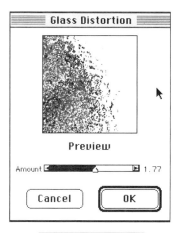

FIGURE 3.49

FIGURE 3.50   GLASS DISTORTION APPLIED ON BACKGROUND WITH VARIOUS PAPER TEXTURES

Motion Blur

This will blur the whole image or a selected portion of it. Use the Polygonal, Freehand, or Stencil tools to select a portion of your image. If an area of your image isn't selected, the whole image will be blurred. A dialog box displays how the Motion Blur image will appear. A slider bar lets you adjust the radius of the blur. Another slider bar adjusts the angle of the motion.

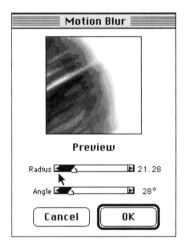

FIGURE 3.51A **MOTION BLUR**

FIGURE 3.51B **MOTION BLUR APPLIED TO A MATADOR'S CAPE**

▪ ▪ ▪ ▪ ▪ ▪ ▪ ▪ ▪ ▪ ▪ ▪

Negative

This effect reverses the colors (changes them to their opposite on the Color Wheel) of the entire image or a selected area. Use the Polygonal, Freehand, or Stencil tools to select a portion of your image. If nothing is selected, the entire image will be effected. Use the **Negative** option a second time to revert the image back to the original.

FIGURE 3.52A　　**INK DRAWING OF A WOMAN**

FIGURE 3.52B　　**NEGATIVE APPLIED TO DRAWING OF A WOMAN**

Sharpen

Use the Polygonal, Freehand, or Stencil tools to select a portion of your image. If nothing is selected, the entire image will be effected. The image will be sharper and more in focus. Textures and lines appear crisper.

FIGURE 3.53 SHARPEN EFFECT WAS APPLIED TO A RECTANGLE IN THE CENTER OF THIS STILL LIFE DRAWING

Soften

Soften gives the image a fuzzy, out-of-focus appearance. Use the Polygonal, Freehand, or Stencil tools to select a portion of your image. If nothing is selected, the entire image will be effected.

FIGURE 3.54 SOFTEN WAS APPLIED TO A FREEHAND STENCIL, OVER THE WOMAN'S SKIRT

Textures   The Textures effect applies the selected paper texture from the Papers drawer. A dialog box shows how the textured image will appear. A slider bar lets you adjust the amount of texture ranging from 0% to 100%.

FIGURE 3.55   TEXTURE APPLIED OVER IMAGE

Plug-in Filters   Lets you apply third-party filters over Polygonal, Freehand, or Stencil areas or over the whole image.

Options Menu

Zoom Factor   Reduces or enlarges the monitor view of your image in increments ranging from 8.3% to 1200% (the Magnifier tool in the Tools drawer gives you the same size intervals as the pop-up menu).

Drawers   The Drawers menu is used for opening and closing Dabbler's drawers. The Drawers option contains a Drawer pull-down menu that lets you select the drawer you want to open. These drawers include Extras, Tools, Colors, and Papers. At the bottom of the list is the Close All Drawers command, which closes all currently opened drawers.

The key commands for the drawers are:

MACINTOSH

Command-1, Extras
Command-2, Tools
Command-3, Colors
Command-4, Papers
Command-H, Close All Drawers

PC

Ctrl-1, Extras
Ctrl-2, Tools
Ctrl-3, Colors
Ctrl-4, Papers
Ctrl-H, Close All Drawers

Draw Freehand	Allows you to draw or paint free-flowing strokes with Dabbler's tools.
Draw Straight Lines	Allows you to draw or paint straight lines with Dabbler's tools. Click once to establish an origin point; click again and a line will appear). To finish a polygon, click on the origin point and press **Enter** on the numeric keypad.
Tracing Paper	Turns the current page semi-transparent, revealing the underlying page in the sketchpad.
Invert Stencil	Lets you draw or fill on outside of a stencil, while temporarily masking the inside of the stencil.
Invert Paper Texture	Inverts selected Paper Texture, making highlights shadows, and shadows highlights.
Text Styles	The Type Styles option dialog box is used to specify the font, and size for your text. Select a font from the top menu, and use the lower slider bar to adjust the size of the font. A sample of the font you've chosen will be displayed in the center box.
	The color of the text will appear as the current color selection in the color palette. The color can be changed as you're typing in text.
	Note that the Text icon must be selected before the Type tool is selected in order for either one to function.
	You can type only one line of text at a time. To start another line of text, reposition the cursor where you want the text to appear. The previous line of text is now part of the background image.

FIGURE 3.56 **THE TYPE SPECIFICATION WINDOW**

Sessions

The **Session** option records and plays back drawing sessions, showing the steps used to create artwork, from start to finish. These sessions are ideal to use as teaching tools, for creating presentations, or as a review for artists to check the steps involved in creating their work.

In the dialog box, click on the **Recorder** icon (the right-facing triangle). Your Tools drawer window will display a scrollable palette, name window, and buttons resembling video cassette recorder buttons.

Flipbook Options

Dabbler's **Flipbook** option let you choose how many Tracing Paper layers (as many as four) will be visible. This option lets you choose how many previous and/or forward pages you want to see. Also included in the Flipbook options is a box that gives you a choice of having your artwork loop when you play back your Flipbook animation. By checking the **Loop Playback** option box, your piece will keep playing until you stop it in the Flipbook controls (see Chapter 4 for more information).

FIGURE 3.57 **THE SESSIONS RECORDER ICONS**

Recording a Session

To record a session, open **Sessions** in the Options menu. The **Record** button (the red circle) and the **Stop** button (the square) appear on the face of the Tools drawer. Click on the **Record** button and begin creating your image. When you're finished with the first step, click on the **Stop** button. A dialog box will appear asking you to name your session. Click **Cancel** if you don't want to save your session.

Playing Back a Session

To play back your session, open a new page, and reopen the Sessions window through the Options menu. Select the session from the scroll palette, and click the Play button (the right-facing triangle). The drawer closes and the session plays. The **Stop**, **Pause**, and **Step** (selecting **Step** will play one stroke at a time) options are also available while the session is playing back.

Sessions can be stopped, added to, and then restarted. One tool remains on the face of the drawer for easy access.

You can also layer sessions over existing drawn or scanned images on Dabbler pages. This layering process can create some very innovative images that can be used as teaching tools or presentations.

Recorded sessions give you a chance to be creative with movement, adding new dimensions to your art. You can even create your own special effects (see Session 28 for more ideas).

Recording Instructions

Another feature of the Recorder utility is the ability to record instructions or supplemental text with the sessions you create. This capability allows artists to give step-by-step instructions throughout the creation process.

To use this feature:

■ Click on the **Sessions Options** from the menu bar, and then select Record Instructions.

- A dialog box opens, allowing you to type up to 256 characters. When you finish typing, press **OK** to begin working on your image.

- When you want to add more text, stop drawing and reselect **Recorder Instructions**. Once again, type text in the dialog box and click **OK**. Continue drawing, repeating this process as often as you wish.

- Click on the **Stop** icon when your session is completed. Name your session in the dialog box, then click **OK**.

When playing back your session, the instructions (text) will appear as they were recorded. You may read the text at your own pace and click OK, and the session will continue in the playback mode.

 **The Recording Instructions capability can be used for other creative projects, such as telling a story where the animation slowly builds, ending with a final, frozen image.**

SESSION LIBRARIES

Being able to create Session Libraries is very useful for organizing your work since they let you separate sessions into groups. Session Libraries can focus on subjects, themes, presentations, individual artwork, galleries, or even a series of session stories.

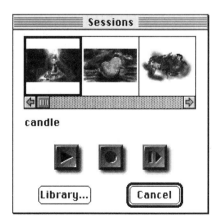

FIGURE 3.58

Opening a Library

To open a Session Library, click on the **Eject** icon. A dialog box will appear allowing you to select a Session Library. Click **Open** to open the selected library. The contents of the selected library will fill the scrollable palette in the Recorder drawer.

Creating a New Library

To create a new Session Library, click on the **Eject** icon, then click on **New**. A dialog box will appear. Type a name for your Session Library in the dialog box, and click OK. Your new, empty Session Library will appear in the scrollable palette. Sessions will be inserted into your new Sessions Library as they are recorded.

Tutors Menu

Dabbler On-Line Manual	The **Dabbler On-Line Manual** selection provides instructions for reaching Dabbler's On-Line Manual with your modem and on-line service. Once you're on-line, you have a choice of reading the manual on-line or downloading it.
Walter Foster Animations	Dabbler provides a series of Walter Foster Sessions and Flipbooks that teach animation lessons by animator/cartoonist Preston Blair. These Sessions teach many of the fundamental basics of animation, such as walking sequences and basic movement.
Walter Foster Cartoons	These are a series of Walter Foster Cartooning Sessions by Bruce Blitz. Sessions include fundamentals of cartooning and structure and development of characters.
Load Others...	This selection lets you access other tutorial sessions.

STENCILS

CLONES

FLIPBOOKS

ADVANCED DABBLER

This chapter covers the following topics:

- Creating New Sketchpads
  - Size
  - Resolution
  - Set Color Paper

▨ Working with Scans

▨ Working with CDs

▨ Working with Clones

▨ Mixed Mediums

▨ Tracing on a Tablet

▨ Working with Stencils

▨ Working with Type

▨ Flipbooks, Animation, and QuickTime Movies

CREATING NEW SKETCHPADS

To create a new Sketchpad, select **Open New Sketchpad** under the File menu. A New Sketchpad dialog box appears.

Enter the **width** and **height** of the Sketchpad image area by selecting your measurement standard from the boxes to the right of the **Measurement** boxes. Enlarging the page size will increase your Sketchpad file size.

You may also set the number of pages in your Sketchpad. You are not limited to number of pages. You may add and delete pages with the **New Page**, **Delete Page**, or **Browse Pages** selections from the Edit menu.

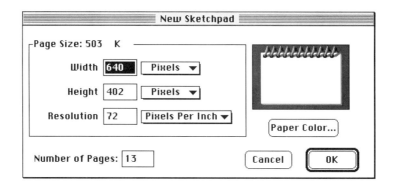

FIGURE 4.1   THE MEASUREMENT BOXES IN THE
NEW SKETCHPAD DIALOG BOX

Resolution

You can change the resolution size of the Sketchpad by typing your specification in the **Resolution** box located in the New Sketchpad dialog box. You have a choice of entering resolution in **pixels per inch** or **pixels per centimeter**.

Resolution │ 72 │ │ **Pixels Per Inch ▼** │

FIGURE 4.2   **THE RESOLUTION BOX IN THE NEW SKETCHPAD DIALOG BOX**

Dabbler's default resolution is 72 pixels per inch, which is standard screen resolution. This setting will work well with most standard laser, dot matrix, and thermal printers. For high-resolution prints or film, you may want to raise the resolution to double that of the lines per inch (lpi) that your output device produces. For example, a four-color printed piece on glossy paper may need to be printed at 133 lines per inch, so you'll want to set Dabbler's resolution to 266 pixels per inch.

Remember, when the resolution is increased, the file size is also increased. If you have limited RAM or hard drive space and your files are large, Dabbler's performance will be slowed.

When creating professional print work, you will need a separate program such as Photoshop to convert Dabbler's RGB (screen colors) files to CMYK (process colors) for printing.

Set Paper Color

Included in the New Sketchpad dialog box is a **Set Paper Color** box for choosing a page color. When a choice is made, the color will appear in the box to the right. The page color you choose will appear on all the pages in that Sketchpad.

Paper Color...

THE SET COLOR PAPER BOX IN THE NEW SKETCHPAD DIALOG BOX

If you want different color pages, select the Set White Paper Color box. Fill each page using Fill from the Edit menu, or a Bucket tool fill when you open a new page.

WORKING WITH SCANS

Scans are digital images produced from photos or art on a scanner. Scanners allow artists to digitize photos and manipulate them in the computer. Dabbler's cloning feature lets you create images from photos that look as though they were painted. Photo scans brought into Dabbler can be drawn on, spray painted, changed with effects, or manipulated in other ways with Dabbler's tools and functions.

To bring a scan into Dabbler it must be in RGB mode and in Photoshop, or another file format that Dabbler accepts (refer to Chapter 3 for more information).

When scanning in color or grayscale, a rule of thumb is to double the resolution of what the final dpi (dots per inch) output will be.

Resolution for most home printers is 150; resolution for process printing on glossy stock is 266 to 300.

N O T E

A simple line drawing scan can serve as a base drawing to be used in many ways:

- As a template to trace from, using Dabbler's Tracing Paper Feature.

- As a base for a Dabbler drawing.

- As reference for laying out final work.

- As a piece that can be manipulated and refined.

There may be times you'll want to scan a piece of art, then bring it into Dabbler to achieve a specific effect. Scanning (like cloning) gives you the opportunity to experiment with a piece of art without changing the original.

Scanned images can also be placed into Dabbler's Flipbooks for animation or QuickTime movies.

WORKING WITH CDs

Photo CDs can provide artists with a tremendous number of images for the computer. They provide both professionals and novices with libraries of subjects, ideas, and scrap material.

One hundred stock photo images are included on the Dabbler CD. Subjects on the Dabbler CD images include **Background, Food, Holidays, Nature, People, Science, Sports,** and **Travel.** These files can be used for experimentation, cloning, photo manipulation, tracing, and as subject matter for sketching.

Commercial CDs are available from stores, mail-order catalogs, and computer exhibits. Images include clip art, cartoons, illustrations, and photos. The price range varies from inexpensive to costly. The quality of the images varies also, and manufacturers have different copyright restrictions. Be sure to read the copyright restrictions, since some CD manufacturers do not allow their images to be used commercially, and others charge royalties.

Kodak's Photo CDs allow you to put your own photos onto CDs. This is a great way to work with your own images and create image libraries.

FIGURE 4.4   FOOD SAMPLE FROM
DABBLER'S CD IMAGES

WORKING WITH CLONES

Cloning is an important and useful feature of Dabbler. By making a clone of an original, you can experiment with an image without changing the original. For example, cloning lets you change the style of your artwork easily by applying different styles of strokes, such as those seen in Figure 4.5.

Refer to Chapter 3 for instructions on how to use Dabbler's Cloning feature.

Cloned photos can be made into paintings or drawings by using Dabbler's different Drawing and Painting tools. For example, a photo of a landscape can be turned into an impressionistic painting by using the Oil Paint tool and the **Impressionistic** selection in the Extras drawer.

A photo of a landscape can be turned into a pointillism painting by using the Ink Bottle tool with the medium size tip (**stippling** selection), as shown in Figure 4.6.

Another application for Dabbler's Cloning utility is to create a clone of an original, then bring back *parts* of the image rather than the whole image.

FIGURE 4.5 **BALBOA PARK CLONE (SEVERAL BRUSH TOOLS WERE USED, AND THE WATER DROP TOOL WAS USED FOR BLENDING)**

FIGURE 4.6   **INK BOTTLE TOOL CLONE**

FIGURE 4.7   SWANS SCAN PARTIALLY CLONED
WITH THE CHALK TOOL

 To create a new impressionistic landscape, use your artwork from Section II, Session 20 with the Cloning utility, the Oil Paint tool, and the **Impressionistic** selection from the Extras drawer.

FIGURE 4.8   THE CLONED IMPRESSIONISTIC VERSION

MIXED MEDIUMS

Dabbler's environment emulates a traditional environment beautifully, while also providing artists with extraordinary advantages. Dabbler is able to combine mediums and tools in new ways to achieve stunning and unusual results. For example, you can use the Water Drop tool to blend strokes laid down by the Oil Paint tool. In Dabbler, oil and water *do* mix!

Another way that Dabbler gives you an advantage over traditional mediums is that you can use the Eraser tool to erase *any* Dabbler medium, including Oil Paint and Ink.

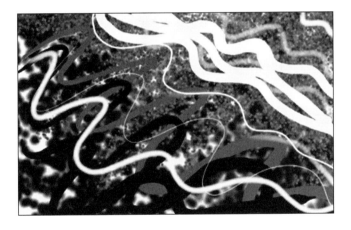

FIGURE 4.9   **THE EFFECT OF USING THE ERASER OVER OIL PAINT AND INK**

TRACING ON A TABLET

One of the reasons pressure-sensitive drawing tablets offer a real advantage over using the mouse or keyboard commands on a computer is that they allow the user to trace a traditional image directly onto a Dabbler page.

When tracing, be sure the image you're tracing from is held firm against the tablet. Many tablets have plastic flip-up overlays that hold artwork in place.

Using the stylus (the pen that comes with the tablet), lightly tap the perimeters of your image to make sure that it fits on your Dabbler page. Once the paper image is set up correctly, start tracing. Check the image on your screen against the image you're tracing from often, and adjust the line weight as needed with increased or decreased pressure from the stylus.

WORKING WITH STENCILS

Dabbler supplies a variety of Stencil Libraries that can be accessed through the Extras drawer when the Stencil tool is selected.

These libraries contain a variety of shapes, animals, symbols, silhouettes, images, and maps. These templates can be incorporated into artwork, educational projects, sessions, and Flipbooks.

FIGURE 4.10   **FOREST WAS CREATED USING IMAGES FROM DABBLER'S STENCIL LIBRARIES**

Following are some examples of how the templates can be used:

▪ In a theme picture (as shown in Figure 4.10).

▪ To create a montage.

▓ For layering Stencils with Fade and other effects.

▓ To distort Stencils with the Liquid tool, Water Drop tool, and effects.

▓ Mixing filled Stencils with drawn-in templates.

FIGURE 4.11 **STENCILS USED IN A VARIETY OF WAYS**

WORKING WITH TYPE

When incorporating type into an image, it's important to carefully choose the font (typeface) you want to use. Consider whether the font accurately conveys the style and mood of the image you're creating, whether it's dainty, bold, romantic, simple, etc.

The placement of type is also an important consideration in the balance of a piece. The placement of type can help steer the viewer through the piece, or lead them to a focal point.

Color, background, placement, font, and font size are all important considerations to take into account when using type in an image.

Interesting effects that can be created with type include:

■ Drop shadows,

■ Angled type (rotate the page to the angle you want and type in your text; then rotate the page to a straight position by holding down the Shift key),

■ Erase and draw over parts of letters.

| FIGURE 4.12 | TYPE AT AN ANGLE, ERASED, DRAWN ON, AND DROP SHADOWS |

FLIPBOOK

The **Flipbook** option is used for creating simple animation pieces and printed flipbooks.

Traditional flipbooks are the basis for modern animation. Each page is called a *frame*. Within the frames are images that change slightly from frame to frame. Traditional animators usually start a piece by drawing the main movements of a character. These are called *keyframes*. After the keyframes are finished, the artist draws the smaller movements connecting one main movement to the next. This is called *inbetweening*.

Traditional animators draw on transparent paper, so that they can see, trace, and change the previous image. They review their work by flipping pages to see how the movement works, checking for smooth transitions between movements.

Dabbler's Flipbooks are based on the way traditional animators work. Flipping pages and working with tracing paper are the key elements in the way Dabbler's Flipbooks function.

In addition to creating traditional flipbooks, Dabbler allows you to create sophisticated animation.

■ You can import images (such as scans and illustrations) into the frames.

■ Any Dabbler tools and effects can be used in the creation of Flipbook art.

■ Finished Flipbooks can be turned into QuickTime movies.

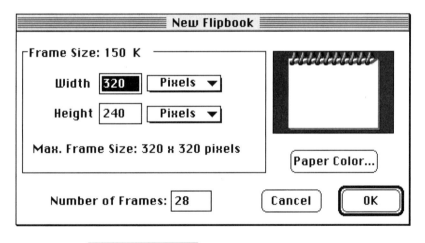

FIGURE 4.13   NEW FLIPBOOK

To create a Flipbook, select **New Flipbook** under the File menu. Type the desired size in the New Flipbook dialog box. The recommended size is **320 pixels by 240 pixels** (which is the size that QuickTime uses; it is the required size for converting Dabbler files into QuickTime files).

In the Flipbook Setup dialog box, type in the resolution. In creating a Flipbook for a computer screen, resolution only needs to be **72 dpi** because that's the resolution shown on a computer screen. Many home printers have low resolution, so 72 dpi will probably work well. For professional printing, you'll want to increase resolution according to your needs.

The Flipbook Setup dialog box lets you customize binding. You can choose to bind from **left**, **right**, **top**, or **bottom**. You may also type in your Binding Width.

 **Plan ahead for how your printed Flipbook should work. The positioning of the character on the pages is very important when deciding on the direction of the binding. How are you going to fasten page frames together—staples, clips, etc.? How much room will you need for binding and for holding the Flipbook?**

The Flipbook Setup dialog box has layout options of **Tiled** and **Single** for printing. **Tiled** puts several frames on a page with rules around the page for cutting. This option saves paper. The **Single** option prints one frame per page. These frames put the image in the same place on each of the pages. This makes it easy to cut out several frames at a time on a paper cutter.

FIGURE 4.14 **FLIPBOOK CONTROL BUTTONS**

When setup is completed, click on the **OK** button. You will be asked to name your Flipbook.

The Flipbook Controls floating menu will also appear on the screen. These options control frame movement.

Flipbook Controls

■ The first button takes you to the beginning of the Flipbook.

■ The second button to the left is the button to turn frames backwards.

■ The square is the **Stop** button.

■ The triangle is the **Play** button.

■ Next to the **Play** button is the **Forward** button.

■ The last button takes you to the end of the Flipbook. This button will automatically create new frames after you've filled all the previous ones.

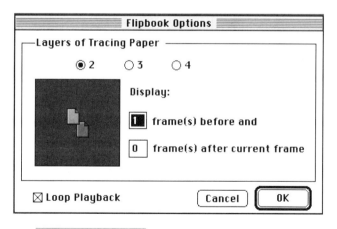

FIGURE 4.15 **FLIPBOOK CONTROLS**

Frames can also be added and deleted through the **Edit** option in the Menu Bar.

In setting up a new Flipbook, you may want to set up tracing layers with the Flipbook Options. To do this, select **Flipbook Options** in the Options menu.

Flipbook Options lets you create as many as four layers of transparency. This enables you to see how your current frame is working with other frames (frames that fall before and/or after the current frame). This feature gives you more control over drawing movement transitions by letting you see several stages of frames changes. When you click on the **Tracing Paper** icon, the Flipbook Options you've set will be displayed on your working frame.

The Flipbook Options dialog box has a box to select **Loop Play**. **Loop Play** keeps your animation running continuously, sending it back to the beginning when the sequence ends. Selecting **Loop Play** continues playing the animated sequence until you press the **Stop** button. If the **Loop Play** box is not selected the animation will stop when it reaches the end of the frames.

Flipbook Options can be changed when you're working on your frames.

Once you've finished setting your Flipbook Options, it's time to think about the artwork you want to create in your Flipbook.

Consider the following elements:

- Is there a theme or story that will interest the viewer?

- Does the character(s) or story lend itself to simple or detailed artwork?

- Is color needed?

- Do the character(s) have enough movement to keep the animation interesting?

 **Black-and-white line art images use less memory than complex color images.**

Saving Frames

Individual frames can be saved by selecting **Save Frame As** from the File menu. A dialog box will ask you to name the document, choose a file format, and select where you want to save it.

Editing Frames

To edit frames, select **Edit** from the Menu Bar.

Add Frames (Command-N)   Adds frames to a Flipbook.

Delete Frames   Deletes frames from a Flipbook.

Browse Frames   Lets you scroll backward and forward through Flipbook frames.

Go to Frame   Each frame is numbered, and this selection lets you open a frame by typing in its number.

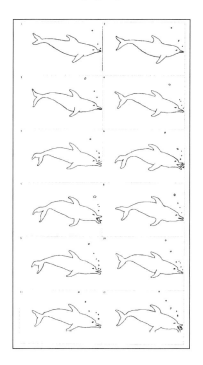

FIGURE 4.16   **DOLPHIN FLIPBOOK PRINTED WITH TILED FORMAT**

QUICKTIME MOVIES

Your finished flipbook animation can be imported into QuickTime by selecting **Export** from the File menu. A pull-down menu will display an **As QuickTime** option.

By making Flipbooks into QuickTime movies, you'll save memory and have the ability to import them into multimedia applications.

SUMMARY

As shown in this chapter, Dabbler has some very advanced features for creating sophisticated images. These features are easy to use and can be incorporated into both novice and professional projects. The following are examples of Dabbler's advanced features:

■ Dabbler's ability to customize Sketchpads gives users the ability to create high-resolution images suitable for commercial printing.

■ Dabbler's tools and cloning capabilities give you infinite creative possibilities when working with CDs and scanned images.

■ Stencil libraries offer images that inspire creativity and ideas for projects. They are also wonderful teaching tools for educators.

■ Type capabilities let you create graphic designs and fine art pieces with type.

■ Dabbler's ability to mix mediums expands an artist's choices well beyond the capabilities of traditional tools.

■ The Flipbook feature lets you create animation and QuickTime movies, putting a new level of exciting capabilities into the hands of Dabbler artists.

FIGURE 4.17   **SCANNED HORSE MANIPULATED WITH SPRAY PAINT, WATER DROP, AND OTHER TOOLS**

SECTION II

SESSIONS

ABOUT THE SESSIONS

This section of *Dabbler* is a series of step-by-step projects that illustrate specific uses of Dabbler's tools, functions, and techniques. These sessions are also designed to cover many of the fundamental principles of art and design, thus providing a fun way of exploring and learning art.

In the beginning sessions you will learn how to use many of Dabbler's tools, along with art concepts and techniques. As the sessions advance, projects combine tools and techniques in more complex projects.

Many advanced sessions use techniques covered in previous sessions. It's important not to skip sessions unless you're a skilled artist and Dabbler user.

In addition to covering skills, the sessions are designed to teach you how to use the process of conceptual thinking and to spark your imagination.

Each session consists of a series of numbered steps. Some sessions include more than one project, and some suggest future projects you can do on your own.

The session art samples may be copied, but I strongly suggest you create your own designs and pick your own subject matter unless otherwise instructed. This will enable you to learn more tools and techniques and gain the experience of choosing subjects that work well for you.

If you decide to copy the sample art, follow up with a piece of your own using the same session and steps.

Many sessions give suggestions, tips, and ideas on where to find reference material for ideas and pictures of subjects. Included with the reference files information are some scanned photos that can be used in different sessions.

REFERENCE FILES

Keeping art files on subjects is very helpful to artists. The more content you have to study and work from, the better your work will be. In creating art files (called a *morgue*), break down subjects into categories such as animals, people, buildings, landscapes, and machines. As the morgue grows it can be broken down into more subcategories. For example, the category of people can be divided into women, men, children, elderly, fashion models, and sports figures.

Computer CDs are another image source. The Dabbler II CD software includes CD images for your use. The CD market is full of wonderful images of numerous subjects available to users. The sample photos provided in this section can be used for reference and as inspirational material for the art sessions.

COPYRIGHTS

When creating art, it's extremely important to follow copyright laws and restrictions. Unless an image source (photo, art, scan, or any other form of image someone else has created) specifies that the image has unlimited usage rights or that the time period of a copyright has expired, it is automatically considered copyrighted. Any published piece is automatically copyrighted.

Because of copyright laws, it's extremely important for an artist drawing images from reference materials (such as a picture in a magazine) to change the image significantly. You can change it from other people by cropping, removing or adding subjects, combining several images, changing colors, and/or applying styles and effects.

Working with photographed images is trickier than with other types of images regarding copyrights. The safest method is to use your own photos or purchase copyright-free CDs.

PENCIL SKETCHES

In traditional art, most artists begin work with a pencil sketch. In Dabbler, I find that creating a pencil sketch using the Pencil tool also works well. Pencil techniques can add textures and styles to drawings. Learning the techniques described in this section is very important because they will be used over and over again.

PENCIL TECHNIQUES

In this exercise, you'll be drawing about 20 circles, so preplan the size and placement of your circles. Don't worry if some overlap slightly (see the sample).

1   In this first part of the session, we will explore a variety of pencil techniques. In the Tool drawer, click on the Pencil and Stencil (first star on the left) tools, then close the Tool drawer. Now your Pencil and Stencil tools are displayed and are available for use.

From the Color drawer, pick a palette with several grays and black. This project involves experimenting with different shades of gray.

Click on the Stencil tool and then on the small left-hand drawer. Click on the circle in the Extra drawer to select it. Hold down the Shift key (this will maintain the shape as a perfect circle), and drag the circle to the drawing surface. Click on the Pencil tool and fill inside the circle with straight lines. Note that the Stencil tool keeps you from drawing outside the circle.

Select the Stencil tool again and draw a second circle. Select the Pencil and change the line width by using the triangles inside the Tool drawer. Repeat the process using different variations of widths and shades of pencil strokes in other circles.

Repeat the process using the following techniques. Remember to use a variety of tip sizes and gray shades.

▪ **Cross-hatching**—cross strokes over one another. In different circles, change the tightness and looseness of strokes.

▪ **Pointillism**—create a series of small dots filling the circle.

▪ Fill the circle with squiggly lines.

▪ From the Paper drawer, select different textures. Experiment with fills from partial pencil to solids, or try several textures in one circle.

▪ Use the Eraser and Water Drop tools to erase, lighten, or smudge pencil drawings in several circles.

Rendering a Pencil Sketch

2 Select a subject that has a variety of lights and darks, textures, and an interesting background.

Select the Pencil tool and a light or medium gray from the Color palette. Adjust the tip to a fine point with the Small Triangle tool in the Tool drawer.

Lightly sketch the outline, main lines, and basic shapes of the subject.

3 At this point, study your subject's *values* (lightness and darkness of colors). Areas that are white or highlighted should remain white (not drawn on). Draw fine details with the small point of the Pencil tool.

Build up shades of gray from the lightest to the darkest areas. Use black in your darkest shadows, dark areas, and to accentuate the dark details. In the duck sample, the eyes, dark feathers, bill, and underneath shadows are emphasized in black. Take a final look at the subject and see if it needs any final details, such as lines distinguishing shapes, textural lines, shadows, and highlights.

4 The final part of this drawing is the background. When creating backgrounds, blend carefully, and don't detract from the main subject matter—it's important not to overdo style.

Some shapes may be shadowed forming silhouettes, such as the blades of grass in Sample 3. Lines, cross-hatching, squiggles, and other techniques help shape images and fill in the background.

 **A series of repeated lines or dots gives artwork a rhythmic or textural appearance.**

TOOLS AND TEXTURES

One of the best ways to understand art is to experiment with different tools. In this session, you will learn how to create a simple abstract, although the real focus is on experimentation with tools and textures.

1 Select the Pen tool and black from the Color palette. Choose the Straight Line under Option in the menu bar (Command-L). With the Pen tool, draw an abstract design by filling up the paper with a variety of enclosed shapes.

2 Using a variety of tools, textures, and color combinations, fill in and around the design you've created.

Try the following:

- Pencil, Chalk, and Crayon tools with different Paper Textures.
- Fill in a couple of shapes with the Paint Bucket tool using a solid color and a graduated fill (select a Graduation palette from the Color drawer).
- Use Brush and Ink tools in various sizes.
- Use stroke techniques learned in Session 1 with tools other than the Pencil tool.

3 Clone image. Select the Polygonal Stencil tool. Create interesting stencil shapes on your abstract image, then select Focus from the Effects menu, with a focus choice from the Extra drawer.

Tap inside the stencil and watch the image change. Next try other focus choices. Repeat the process using the Polygonal Stencil tool with the Surface Texture effect and Textures from the Texture drawer. Try using the Negative effect. Use the Float tool to move stencil selected area.

4 Now create a reverse image of your previous artwork, by saving the image with a new name. Select the whole image (use Command-A on the Macintosh, and Control-A on the PC), then click inside using Negative from the effects menu.

ABSTRACTION AND DESIGN PRINCIPLES

Abstract art gives the artist a chance to experiment. This process helps you form design skills, become familiar with the tools, and learn color, shape, balance, and relationships.

1 **Asymmetry**

Asymmetrical design is the result of forms on opposite sides of the center vertical axis being different. Create a simple asymmetrical design by using lines and shapes. Tool and colors are your choice.

2 Create an abstract subject from your last piece or a new piece. For example, create a person, flower, animal, etc. Keep it simple, using only important details. Tool and colors are your choice.

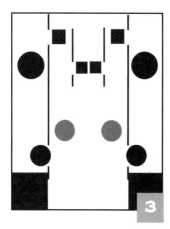

3 Symmetry

A symmetrical design results when forms on opposite sides of the center vertical axis are identical in composition. Create a simple symmetrical design using lines and shapes. All tools and colors are your choice.

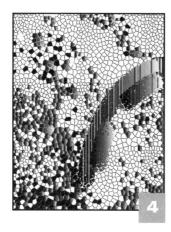

4 Free-Form Abstraction

Create a textural background using the Chalk tool and one or more Paper Textures.

Brush several large strokes with the Brush tool over the textured background. Select the Paint Bucket and fill areas of background and brush strokes. Try both Solid Color and Graduated fills. Leave some areas clear for contrast.

Visualize a loose idea of the finished artwork. Think about the best placement of objects on the page and how they should relate to one another. Is the balance interesting and pleasing?

LINES

Everything around you consists of lines. Objects may be composed of edges or a network of small lines, such as the veins in leaves. When creating art, we look at the straight and curved lines that make up an object's appearance and then integrate them into a drawing. You will need a single flower as the subject of this session.

1 **Directional Lines**

With a light gray fine-point Pencil tool, draw the directional lines of the main parts of the flower. In the daffodil in Sample 1, the directional lines are angles of the stem and leaves that move from the bottom toward the top of the page. Directional lines also radiate out from the center of the flower to the end of the petals.

2 **Outlines**

After finishing your directional lines, find the outlines of the main shapes. In the stalk and leaves, outlines are straight or slightly curved. The petals are arced curves coming together to form a point at the tip. (In Sample 2, the curve was drawn past the tip to show you the arc. It's not necessary to draw that.) The center section is a curved line that forms a circle, which contains a second circle where the ridge bends.

3 Detail and Emphasis Lines

In this step, look for the lines inside the shapes that make up your subject—For example, the lines inside the petals and leaves or the outlines of the shades. Vary the Pencil tool's width and gray tones by priority. Next, draw in some of the key details, such as the parts in the center of the flower and the scalloped edge on the circle, and then emphasize key features and lines using a darker shade of gray.

Contemplate the directions and emphasis of your lines. Do they help guide your eyes through a piece?

SHAPES

In this session you will learn how shapes form subjects. For this session you will need a high-contrast photo of a mammal's face. We use a high-contrast image to show easily see how using lights and darks form shapes that are easy to see.

1. Use a gray fine-tip Pencil tool to break your subject into shapes as you look for the most obvious first—the head, body, and limbs. The face has a number of shapes. In the calf in Sample 1, the base of the nose is triangular and the bridge is rectanglular; the eyes are circles with a straight edge where the lid is; the muzzle is a circle, etc. The calf's upper torso is also broken into several large shapes.

2. In Sample 2, detail and emphasis are added to the shapes. Use a darker shade of gray when adding some emphasis lines.

3 Examine your subject's shadows; many will form very distinctive shapes. Sketch in these shadows to finalize your drawing.

4 In this step, you will create a separate piece of stylized art by accentuating the shapes through black and white contrast. To create this artwork without destroying your previous piece, create a tracing paper as shown in Chapter 4. On your tracing paper, use the Pen tool with a small tip and pick black from the Color palette. Turn on Straight Line (Command-L) and trace your previous drawing, simplifying it into basic enclosed shapes. After drawing each shape, press the Enter key or your shapes will connect. When you finish drawing the shapes, change to the Bucket tool and fill each shape with black.

LIGHT AND SHADOW

Light and shadow add realism and a three-dimensional appearance to artwork. Drama and mood effects can be achieved with light and shadow. If possible, set up a ball with a desk lamp lighting it off to one side. For Sample 2, some round fruits with stems will be needed.

1   Use the Stencil tool to choose Circle and place a medium-size circle (constrain by holding down the Shift key) near the center of the page. Then switch to the Spray Paint tool, using light gray and a large tip.

The first step in illustrating light and shadow is to establish the light source and its direction. Decide in which direction you want your dominant light. Think about how and where it will hit the object. Lightly spray the areas that will be shaded. Tones radiate from light to dark on the round surface. Slowly build up darker areas by changing to darker shades of gray. Lightly spray the background, leaving areas white where the light streams down. Finishing details include:

▪   A "hot spot," where the light hits the object the strongest. Use the Eraser tool to place this.

■ Reflective light may be bouncing up from the table surface. Create this with a small tip on the Spray Paint tool.

■ Shadows on the table surface appear in the opposite direction from the light source.

2 Set fruit on a light color surface near your computer. Take a minute to study the fruit. How do light and shadow affect the surfaces and forms? Notice how color gets gradually darker as it moves away from the hot spot. With the gray Pencil tool, draw a simple line sketch of fruit with stems.

3 Use the Spray Paint tool to shade the fruit. Pick and blend colors carefully as you apply lessons learned from shading the ball in Sample 1. The fruit's surface is not perfectly round, so highlights and shadows will vary more; there may be multiple highlights.

4   Using the Pencil tool, choose a dark tone or black to shade the stems and the area where they connect to the fruit.

5   With a small or medium tip on the Spray Paint tool, darken the underneath areas of the fruit and apply shadows to the surface on its base. Some slight light or color may bounce back into the surface shadow from the fruit.

Further Practice Suggestions: Draw an assortment of objects under different lighting.

SIMPLIFYING SUBJECTS INTO MOTIF IMAGES

Find an image of a bird whose form can be broken down into simple shapes.

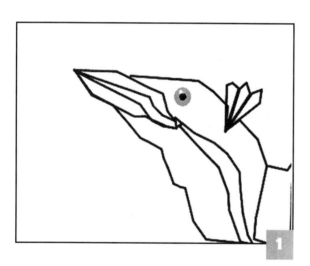

1 Under Options in the menu bar, select Draw Straight Lines. (Remember to press the Enter key when you want lines to break.) Create an outline of the bird and draw the inner shapes, using the Pen tool with black selected. It's okay to simplify the shapes.

Locate the position of the eye. Using the Stencil tool, select a circle in the Extras drawer, drag out a circle; then fill using the Paint Bucket tool. Repeat the process if the pupil, highlight, or other eye is shown. Click in selected stencil to reposition

2   Use Draw Straight Lines and the Pen tool to create an interesting background that complements the style of your bird. Think ahead now to what colors you want to use. They can be different from the bird's real colors; bright colors contrasting with some darks work well.

Turn back to the Freehand tool and switch to the Paint Bucket. On the left side of the Color drawer are the Solid Fill palettes, and on the right side are the Graduated palettes. Use both the Solid Fills and the Graduated Fills, creating your Background Fills last.

3   With the Paint Bucket tool, fill in background shapes. It's important to pick colors that work with the bird's image, and that don't detract or overpower it. Add final details, such as emphasis lines (as shown around the eye in Sample 3); new shapes can also be added for balance or interest.

See the color image in the Gallery.

STENCIL FILLS

Stencils allow the artist to draw within or outside a shape, temporarily masking the area not selected.

1 Use the Graduated Fill palette with the Paint Bucket tool, and fill in the whole drawing area (just click and the whole drawing area will fill). Next, select the Stencil tool and click on the Star in the Extras drawer. Create a star design with stars in a variety of sizes and fills. Fill the stars, using both the drawing tools with textures and the Paint Bucket tool. Stars can be overlapped, stretched, or kept proportional by holding down the Shift key.

2 Select the Polygonal Stencil tool. Draw interesting shapes around the stars and fill them with the Spray Paint tool, as in Sample 2; deselect when you want to begin a new shape. Add as many stars as you'd like.

Deselect by using Command-D for the Macintosh or Ctrl-D for PC.

STENCIL COLLAGE

In this session, the topic is things in the garden. You turn objects from the garden (e.g., leaves) into simple graphic forms. These images combine with geometric forms to create a graphic collage.

Reference Materials: Look at samples of native art and Matisse collage artwork.

3   Use the Polygonal Stencil tool to create a brightly colored background shape. With the Freehand and Polygonal Stencil tools and the Paint Bucket tool, draw simplified leaves, butterflies, or other garden objects in a variety of vivid colors. Layer different objects. Add a few medium-size geometric shapes (Circle and Polygon selections) for balance and detail.

4   Study your artwork's balance, colors, and contrast. Would a few additional key shapes help the composition? If so, use the Stencil and Paint Bucket tools fill techniques.

5   Embellish your image with a few small geometric shapes but don't overdo it! Before adding any final detail, save a copy of the screen version, so that you can come back to it. Step a few feet away from your monitor and look at the image you finished in Sample 5.

6   Study the piece carefully. It may or may not need further work. Then sit down again in front of your work and examine the following:

- ▪   Is it balanced?
- ▪   Is there enough detail?
- ▪   Do the colors work together?
- ▪   Is the subject matter interesting or does it need more items incorporated into the design?

These questions will help you decide what is needed to finish the artwork. See the final color image in the Gallery.

REPETITION

Repetition is an important visual element in composition. In using repetition, an artist can create patterns and give visual dominance to the shape/subject/line or achieve harmony in the likeness.

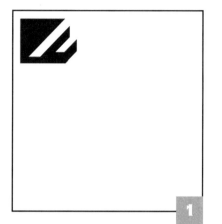

1 Use the polygonal Stencil tool to create a simple polygon shape that takes up about one-eighth of the page. With the Paint Bucket tool and black selected, fill your Polygon design (see Sample 1). Keep your stencil image selected.

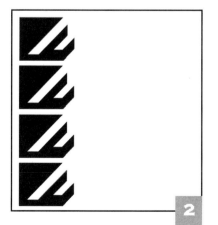

2 Under Edit, select Copy and Paste. Then move the new image to where you want it. Repeat two more times, but leave a section of the page untouched.

Constrain polygon stencil edges to 90 degrees and 45 degrees by holding down the Shift key.

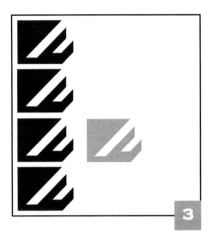

3   Paste and move the image to the untouched area. Make sure you place it where it visually complements the rest of the composition. Keep the image selected and fill it with your color choice, using the Paint Bucket.

REPETITIVE SHAPES FORMING A PATTERN

4   Use the Polygonal Stencil tool to create a simple four-sided polygon in the left-hand corner of the page. With the Paint Bucket tool and a Graduated Fill selected, fill your design. Keep your stencil image selected. Hold down the Option key, click and drag to make a copy of shape. Move it slightly to the right of first shape (see Sample 1). Repeat this process and place the shapes across the top of the page.

5 Copy and paste the shapes (Option key and drag) in a row below the top row. Starting from left to right, use one less than in the previous row, as seen in Sample 5.

6 Continue this process to the bottom of the page. Notice how the shapes form a pattern and break the page into two large positive and negative spaces.

DESIGNING TYPE

Words and letter forms function as wonderful, effective elements in creating designs. Most graphic designers focus on type design or typography.

Reference Materials: Find samples in graphic art annuals, typography books, poster art, and books on the Dadaist art movement.

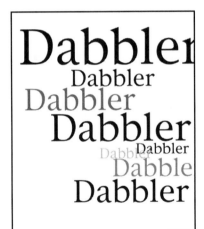

1 Choose a word you like or your name. Select the Text tool and Type Style in the Options menu. When you select TypeStyle, a box opens, allowing you to choose a typeface and to adjust the type size on a Slider bar. Type your word in black or grays, in one typeface, so that you can concentrate on the design, without having to focus on the colors and fonts. Place various character sizes of your word on the page. Consider the overall design and balance when laying out your words.

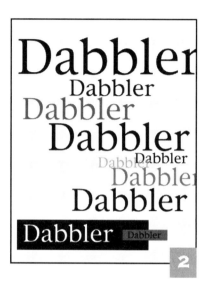

2 Use the Stencil tool to select the Square and add a black rectangle large enough to fit your word. Use the Paint Bucket tool to fill the rectangle. Then change to the Text tool with white selected, and place your word over the rectangle. When deciding where to put the rectangle, remember that it will be the focal point; other rectangles with type may be added at your discretion (see Sample 2).

INCORPORATING TYPE WITH GRAPHIC ELEMENTS

Use a word that's an action word or a subject that's interesting to you. When choosing, think about simple design elements that give the idea of the word without being too pictorial. In Sample 5, the squiggle gives the viewer the idea of art.

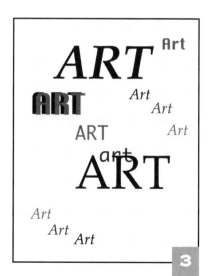

3 Using the Text tool and Type Style option, input your word. Use different fonts and colors in this session. You can layer a light word over a dark word to form a drop shadow effect, as seen in Sample 3. Arrange type in a way that leaves room for design elements that will be added later.

4   Add elements that visually hold your words together. These elements can be borders, shapes, and rules.

5   Add to the mood or meaning of your word with simple graphic elements. In Sample 5, the handwritten word, the squiggle, and the rules leading from the words to the artistic graphic on the side add the concept of art to the piece.

DRAWING WITH INK

Black India ink has its own wonderful line quality, and Dabbler emulates this perfectly. In this session, the subject matter should have some movement to it.

1 Use the Ink tool in black with the Small Tip selected. In this drawing, you want to draw the essence and movement of the subject. In Sample 1, draw the gestures, movements, and key elements of the figure. Keep lines fluid and loose.

2 Add color using loose strokes, with some white showing as highlights. Next, add black descriptive detailing, keeping the same feel to the brush strokes. Adding more hair and outlining the umbrella were all the details that were needed in Sample 2.

BRUSHES

Dabbler's Brush tool allows the user to paint in numerous styles. This session shows you how a painting can be done in one style and then simply changed to a different style. Use pictures of cactus in desert scenes for reference.

Reference: The more you see how other artists paint, the more techniques you will be able to pick up. Visit art galleries and museums, and look at books featuring painters or styles.

1 With the Paint Bucket tool, fill in a colored background. Using the Brush tool, and changing the tip size accordingly, draw in the basic shapes of the cactus. You can reference from several pictures as needed.

2   Use the Brush tool to add more colors inside the cactus borders. Leave white highlights where they are shown. Fill in the centers of any cactus flowers.

3   Change the Brush tool to black and select a fine tip. Add black lines and dot strokes on the shadowed areas of the cacti.

4   Using the Brush tool, create a stylized background. Add hills with long, sweeping strokes and spiral strokes for the sun and sky. A black silhouette of a cactus adds depth and interest to the background. Using complementary colors (opposite colors on the color wheel) adds vibrancy. Save the artwork. See this image in color in the Gallery.

5   Clone image 4. Switch to the Water Drop tool with a fine tip. Lightly blend the colors in the cactus. Leave some of the black outlines solid.

6 Blend the background hills and sky, and do a final blending of the cactus if needed. Save your cloned image.

 **Use the Clone function to create variations of a piece.**

STIPPLING

Delicate detail can be achieved with stippling techniques, which are explained in this session.

1 Sketch a flower blossom with a gray Pencil tool. (The blossom sketch should fill most of the page.) Create Tracing Paper so pencil lines won't show on final art. Change to the Ink Bottle tool at the middle tip and select black from the Color palette. Lightly fill in the main shapes and shadows, and use the Eraser tool for cleaning up any dot overspray.

2 Use the Ink Bottle tool to add details to the stem and petals. Also build up shadows and add definition to shapes.

FIGURE DRAWING

Proper proportions and placement of limbs are the most important parts of drawing figures. Photos of both men and women standing will be needed for the first exercise.

Reference Materials: Photos and drawn or painted images of people.

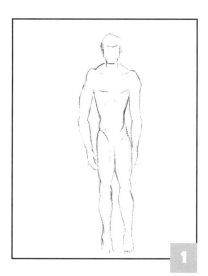

1

1. Use the gray Pencil tool with a small tip to draw the male figure. Pretend a cord runs through the middle of the body. Draw it lightly using a light gray Pencil tool. (In different positions, the imaginary cord bends with the body.) Next, using simple Pencil tool lines, draw the position of the head, rib cage, arms, and legs. When arms are held straight down at a person's sides the fingertips will hit at midthigh. Lightly draw feet and hands, starting with simple shapes. Leave fingers, toes, and other details until the end. Slowly build body mass and darken the outline. Male figures are usually muscular and broad through the shoulders, but small at the hips.

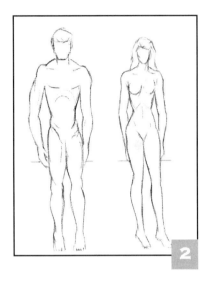

2 Use the gray Pencil tool. Females are curvier—having a waistline, breasts, and wide hips—in comparison to the male body; the rib cage and shoulders are smaller. As with men, women's arms held straight down hit at midthigh. Women's features are usually softer, and they have finer fingers, toes, and bone structure.

FIGURES IN MOTION

Use photos or your own sketches of people in motion poses. Dancers or sports figures work well.

3 With a fine-tip, light gray pencil, draw motion and directional lines of the torso, arms, and legs.

4   As the body twists, it's important to draw the tilt of the shoulders, rib cage, and hips. Start adding form to the body and position the hands and feet where they belong.

5   Darken with the black Pencil tool to add more descriptive detail to the hands, feet, and outline of the body. Use clean, smooth strokes.

6 Draw facial features, clothing, and shadows within the figure. A black Pen tool can be used in areas that need a solid black. Use the Eraser tool for cleaning edges, erasing unwanted lines, and adding highlights. Also add shadows on the ground. Save your drawing.

7 Create a Tracing Paper for your Sample 4 figure. Using a fine-tip black Pen tool, trace your outline and fill it using the Paint Bucket tool. Switch back to the Pen tool for any touch-up work that's needed (such as those white areas that the Paint Bucket tool didn't fill). You have created a silhouette by completely shadowing the body within the outline.

Many beginning artists draw hands and feet that are too small. Look closely at their size in relation to other parts of the body.

PORTRAITS: DETAILING EYES

Well-drawn eyes are imperative to create a good portrait. When eyes are not drawn correctly, they are usually the first feature the viewer notices, making the whole image look off-balance.

Reference Material: Fashion magazines (especially make-up ads) are an excellent reference material for eyes. Practice drawing eyes in different positions—sideways, three-quarters, partially closed, and so on.

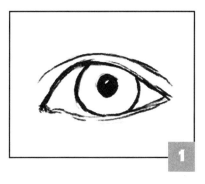

1   Start drawing with a gray, fine-tip Pencil tool. Draw the basic structure of the eye. The breakdown of the eye is an eyeball, eyelid, lashes, and a tear duct. The eyeball contains a retina and pupil. Look closely at the shape of the eye and how its parts are positioned. Refer to Sample 1.

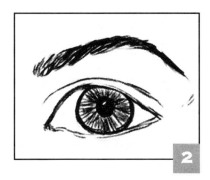

2   Now add detail to the retina. Using the Pencil tool, draw soft lines that radiate out from the pupil to the ring of the retina. Next draw the eyebrow. Note how the hairs toward the center of the face should move upward and outward. Some should lay horizontal and some downward as they progress to the side.

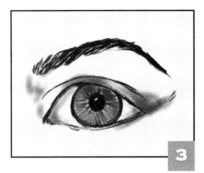

3   At this point, change to the smallest tip of the Spray Paint tool. Pick gray and add shadows that give the eye and eyeball a round shape. The top lid usually causes a slight shadow to fall onto the eyeball.

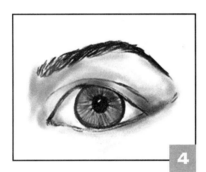

4   Next pick colors for the retina. Lightly spray them with the Spray Paint tool while letting some of the underlying detail show through. Continuing with the Spray Paint tool, add fleshy colors around the eye. Also add tints of orange for warmth, while keeping highlighted areas on and above the lid.

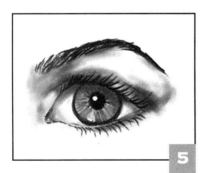

5   This is the final detailing step. At this phase, it is easy to overdo or make mistakes, so you may want to select all, and cut and paste into another page in order to save your previous art. With the Spray Paint tool, continue shaping the surface with more shadows, highlights, and color. The round, glassy shape of the eyeball is accentuated by highlights and shadows. With a small Eraser tool add a white dot slightly off center in the pupil. This makes the eye appear more round, lively, and realistic.

The final touch is the lashes, which are drawn with a small-tip Pencil tool. All the lashes should be drawn in one direction, from the edge of the eyelid outward. Try and keep a soft touch while drawing the lashes, so they don't look overdone or heavy. See the finished color image in the Gallery.

PORTRAITS

Faces consist of a combination of flat and curved planes that make up a three-dimensional shape. Light hits these planes, creating highlights and shadows. Features, hair, and identifying details combine to make a portrait.

In this session, portraits will be created in grays and black so that the user can concentrate on the structure of the face without having to learn color at the same time. Color samples are shown later in the Gallery.

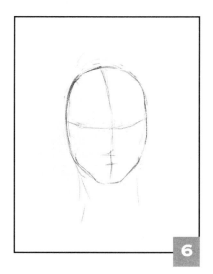

6 Using the gray, fine-tip Pencil tool, lightly sketch the general shape of the face. Heads are somewhat egg-shaped and slightly smaller through the jawline. Sketch in the lines positioning the eyes, nose, and mouth. The eyes are halfway between the top and bottom of the head. The nose is about halfway between the eyes and the bottom of the chin.

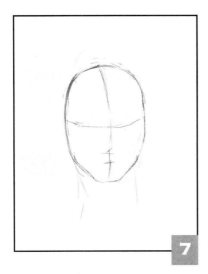

7 Sketch in the eyes, nose, mouth, and eyebrows. (At this point, draw the features as line shapes; shading, shadows, and details will come later.) The pupils roughly line up with the corners of the mouth.

8 Next, lightly sketch the shape of the hair. Not every strand needs to be drawn! Hair should be drawn as shapes with detail at the part line, where it changes direction, and a few wisps around bangs and edges. Sketch the placement of main shadows.

9   Use the Chalk tool for coloring hair. It's important to draw shadows and highlights. Many times, the part line and underneath hair, especially around the nape of the neck, are shadowed. Some of these areas may be drawn as fairly solid black shapes. Highlights generally hit the top of the head outside the part area and the area where the directional light hits. Add shadow from light to dark. Darken the eyes, lips, and eyebrows.

With a dark gray Pencil tool, define features in more detail.

■   Lips "V" down slightly where the canal from the nose comes down. The crease where the lips meet is dark and shadowed. The top lip is usually shadowed more than the bottom. Lips usually have reflective highlights.

■   When drawing the nose, look at the highlights and shadows that define its shape. Don't neglect detailing the nostrils—this is important in defining the nose.

1O   Use the Water Drop tool to blend colors and shadows. Adjust the tip size accordingly. Refer to Gallery for tips on drawing color portraits.

PROFILES

With profiles, it's important to keep the features in the right place. For example, eyes are drawn halfway down the face. Follow photos of a female and male as you draw.

11 With a fine-tip gray Pencil tool, lightly sketch in placement of features, chin, ear, neck, and basic shape of the hair. When you finish with the placement of the features, start drawing in darker, more distinctive details. An eye in profile will look triangular with a slight curve to the front of the eyeball. When drawing a female profile, you may want to slightly emphasize the lips and eyelashes.

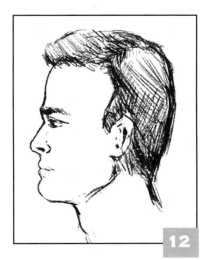

12 With a fine-tip gray Pencil tool repeat the previous process, but add such male characteristics as a strong chin, jawline, neck, and heavy eyebrows. De-emphasize lips and eyelashes. Study the hairline and sideburns of your subject; these vary greatly in men.

ANIMALS

Animals are wonderful subjects because of their variety. The following silhouette exercises help develop your skills in hand-to-eye coordination, spatial interpretation, and interrupting form.

Reference Materials: Collect pictures of reptiles, mammals, and animals in interesting poses.

1 In this first project, try and re-create the horse silhouette in Sample 1.

With the Pencil tool, sketch out the horse. Change to the black Pen tool and outline the animal's form. Fill in the solid areas with the Paint Bucket tool and use the Pen tool for touch-up.

Next, pick an animal image to draw that has an interesting outline. This image may be of an animal in motion, stretching, or flailing its appendages. Follow the steps you used in drawing the horse.

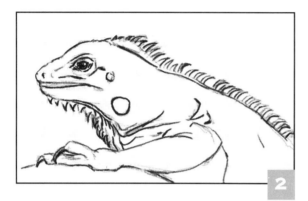

2 Find a picture of a scaly reptile for your subject. With a small-tip gray Pencil tool, sketch your subject.

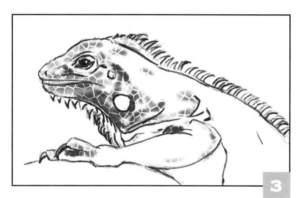

3 Change to the Chalk tool and pick a paper texture that resembles the scales on your subject. (Lizard texture was used in Sample 3.) Pick a medium-light color or gray tone. Start out light and slowly build up to darker shades.

4 Change paper texture if needed, as seen in Sample 4 (Rawhide texture was used). Apply darker shadows. Change to the Spray Paint and select white. Lightly draw in highlights. Switch to the fine-tip black Pen tool, add definition to lines, and accentuate focal areas.

FURRY ANIMALS

Fur is fascinating to draw and is a wonderful method of the study in texture. It comes in a vast array of textures, lengths, and colors.

Re-create the sample art of the koala in Samples 6 through 9. After finishing the koala, repeat this project with your own picture of a furry animal.

5 Do a simple sketch of the koala/animal using the Pencil tool with a fine tip and gray selected.

6 Darken key features of the animal using the Pen tool and the Water Drop tool. In the case of the koala in Sample 6, these are the ears, face, paw, and main fur fringes. The reason these areas are worked on first is because fur is partially over or around them. The Spray Paint you'll be using is a transparent medium, so with light spraying underneath, drawings can be seen.

7   Use the Spray Paint tool to create the koala's fur. Koalas have very soft, fluffy fur, so it's important to keep the edges soft. Spray in large areas of fur, first using a large tip and then progressing to a medium tip for slight details in the fur. Use the small tip for the most detailed area of the fur. Build up color and shadow with layered strokes.

8   In this step, we add the tree branches; the bark and leaves give a nice contrast in texture against the fur of the koala. Use the Pencil and Ink tools to draw in the bark outlines, main textural lines in the bark, and the fill of the leaves.

9   Draw on the bark using the Chalk tool with a gritty texture or two. Leave some highlights. With the Spray Paint tool, add darker shadows on the lower part of the koala's body where he's sitting against the tree. Use the Water Drop to smudge some of the shadows on the bark.

PLANTS

Plants and flowers have been beautiful subjects for millions of artist for thousands of years. They come in vast colors, shape, sizes, textures, and so on. Some plants or parts of plants are symmetrical; others are asymmetrical.

1 Flowers can be drawn with many tools and in numerous styles. Start with a photo of several flower blossoms with some stems and leaves attached. Use a gray Pencil tool with a fine tip to sketch in your image.

2 With the Spray Paint tool, draw a light coat of base color on the subject and the background, leaving highlights white. Change the tip size accordingly.

3   Study the folds, edges, and shapes of your subject, then, still using the Spray Paint tool, add descriptive detail to the leaves, stems, and flowers. Slowly build up shadows.

4   Darken main shadows; a little violet or blue added to the shadows can complement a piece. Add fine details to edges using the Pencil and Pen tools. Slight smudging can be done where needed with the Water Drop tool. Draw in *hot spots* (areas of highest-intensity illumination) and highlights with the Eraser tool. See the finished color image in the Gallery.

5   Garden Scene

Use a photo of a garden, preferably with a wall, pots, deck, and/or walkway. Start by drawing a simple sketch of the scene. Don't put in too much detail—that will come later. With the Paint Brush tool and a large tip selected, put a light base coat in the background and large areas.

6 With the Brush tool and medium and small tips, start applying strokes to the sky and background foliage. Concentrate on general shapes and color so the strokes can be fairly loose. Next, start shaping midsize objects in the middle ground of the image.

Any straight lines, such as in the patio flooring in Sample 6, can be put in with the Pen tool and Straight Line selected.

7 Using the Brush and Pen tools, start putting in small items and fore-ground. Different plants have differ-ent-shaped foliage, so individualize each. The potted plants in Sample 7 show these differences.

8   In this last image, you need to build up colors, shadows, and highlights and to add embellishments. Use the Brush, Water Drop, and Pen tools to mold together the pieces of your scene. On the tiling in Sample 8, the Brush and Pen tools were used to add layers of colors in a stroked pattern. White strokes were then applied, giving the feeling of strong sunlight and luster. Dark shadows and white highlights were applied throughout the scene.

Distinguishing characteristics were applied to flowers, while more strokes and smudging were used in the background to tie in the foreground.

In drawing a garden scene, concentrate on the shapes, textures, and lighting and how they play off one another in the composition.

FISH

Fish have personalities from scary to humorous, making them interesting subjects to draw.

1 This first set of drawings will be of a spotted eel. If you can find a picture of an eel, feel free to use it; if not, copy the eel in Sample 1, but try to change it with the body angling differently or the face looking in another direction. Start with a simple sketch using the gray Pencil tool.

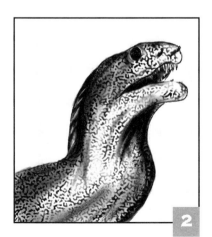

2 Select Cowhide texture and the Chalk tool with a wide tip. Draw texture where its most visible. Shades will vary. Study the image sample to see where lights and darks lay. After you finish the texture, switch to the Spray Paint tool. Place the shadows with a fine tip, and add color to the inside of the eel's mouth.

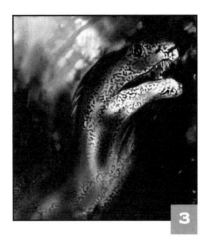

3 Create a background environment using the large Chalk tool with the Globes texture selected. In the background and the back parts of the eel, lightly smudge and blend with the Water Drop tool.

4 Use a color reference photo of a brightly colored fish. Use the gray small-tip Pencil tool to create a simple drawing.

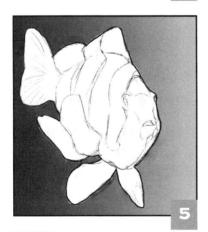

5 Using a heavier black Pencil tool, draw a dark outline around the fish. Make sure the outline is solid. Select a Graduation Color palette for the water. Change colors if you wish, by selecting the boxes on each end of your Graduated palette and choose new colors from the color wheel. Select the Paint Bucket tool and fill in the background.

6 Color the fish using the Spray Paint tool. Start with the large areas first and work down to the small parts. Adjust your spray size accordingly, adding in lights and shadows. Using the Pen tool, fill in the dark part of the eyes, and add emphasis lines where needed.

7 Change to the Chalk tool and pick a texture that looks like fins. Choose a tint of each color or white, and lightly draw on scales where they are the most visible. Next, add bone structure definition to the fins and tail using the small-tipped Eraser tool. The final touch is a few bubbles, also created with the Eraser tool. Keep them round and varied in size. See the finished color image in the Gallery.

PERSPECTIVE

Depth and dimension are illustrated with perspective.

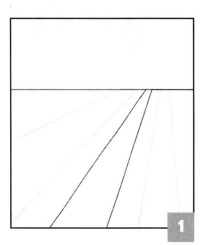

1 Create a horizon line using the gray Pencil tool with the Straight Line selected. The horizon line creates a plane and keeps objects from floating. Create a point slightly above the horizon line. This is your *vanishing point*. From this point, draw a line, with Straight Line selected, to the lower edge of your image area (press the Enter key to break the line, so it won't connect to the next line). Draw another line a couple of inches over on the bottom back to the vanishing point. With the Eraser tool, erase the area above the horizon. This is an example of two parallel lines in perspective meeting at a vanishing point.

2 Next, create a road using the Paint Bucket tool with black selected. Fill between the two lines you've just drawn. Do you see how your image looks like a road vanishing in the distance? Before creating a row of palm trees on each side of the road, draw light lines to your vanishing point to show where your trees will be drawn. Then draw lines showing the placement of the base of the palm trees.

3 Use the Pencil and/or Pen tool to draw the palm trees. Apply the following rules of perspective in creating your palms:

■ Similar-sized objects get smaller as they go toward the horizon.

■ The closer an object is, the more detail it will have. The further the object, the fewer the details.

■ Distant objects are seen frequently as silhouettes.

4 Create a sky with the Pen tool and use the Water Drop tool for smudging. The brightest part of the sky will be your light source. With the Pen tool, draw the hills. The distant hills are filled in with black, as silhouettes.

Draw a pyramid showing two sides. Draw detailed palm fronds (leaves) in the foreground. Having something in the foreground adds comparative depth as well as interest to the composition. Considering the directions of your light source, add shadows and highlights throughout your landscape.

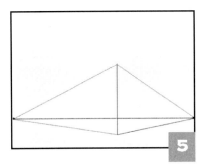

5 Create a city scene using the following two-point perspective method.
Create a straight horizon line using
the gray Pencil tool and the Straight
Line selected. Put dots at the ends of
the horizon line. Draw a vertical line
through your horizon line. From the
top of this line, connect the two
points at opposite ends of the horizon line. From the bottom of your
vertical line, connect lines to the two
outward points.

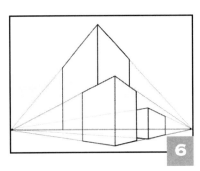

6 The vertical line you drew is the corner edge of a building. Draw a vertical line to the left and right of the
previous vertical line. Make sure the
lines start and end on the diagonal
lines that are connected to your two
points. These are the building's
edges, so think carefully about the
width of your building. Add new
shapes to these structures by repeating the process with different heights
at the corner building's vertical lines.

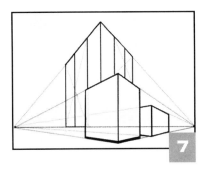

7 Go over the final building lines with
the black Pen tool as shown in
Sample 7. Add vertical windows to
one of the buildings. The windows
will be slightly smaller as their distance from the forward corner
increases.

8 Add doors to the buildings. The top of the door should run along a line from the perspective point. Using the Pen tool, outline the door in black. With the Pen and Spray Paint tool, draw in trees, plants, the sky, and sidewalks. With the Spray Paint tool, put in shadows, highlights, and reflections on the glass of the buildings.

LANDSCAPES

Nature gives artists limitless inspiration for landscapes. Learning to paint a variety of terrains improves an artist's way of seeing the interrelationship of color, texture, shapes, and light. Begin a folder of landscape photos that includes pictures of deserts, mountains, rolling hills, and barns or buildings; add other landscape photos that show a person or two and animals as well.

Reference Material: *National Geographic* and *Arizona Highways* are two of the best nature sources available.

1 Find an interesting mountain scene with an animal or tree in the foreground. Draw a horizon line across the paper above or below the center. Next, using the Pencil tool, draw in the main shapes.

2   Using the Spray Paint tool, place a light undercoat of color in the large areas; areas that are white stay white. Make the top corners of the sky slightly darker.

3   Select the Chalk tool and start drawing in large areas. Choose textures that complement what you are drawing. For example, rough texture is appropriate for the mountain areas.

If you have any smooth water in your image, switch to the Spray Paint tool to get a glassier look. Background objects may be painted softer colors or silhouetted.

4 With the Chalk tool, start darkening shadows and defining areas of the landscape. Add more color to the foreground areas. With the Eraser tool, bring a few main highlights into the image. In Sample 4, highlights are used in the water and snowy areas. Using the Water Drop tool sparingly, smudge the pencil lines at the tops of the mountains, the shadows, and ripples in the water.

5 Using the Pen and Chalk tools, add more details and definition to the foreground, as seen in Sample 5. When you've finished the foreground, look at your whole image. It's easy to overwork a piece at this point, so make sure any new additions or changes are well thought out. This image was completed by adding a few more white highlights in the snow, using the Eraser tool. A few shadows were smudged using the Water Drop tool. See the finished color image in the Gallery.

6 Use a picture of a barn or old building on a road, with some foothills around it. Sketch the scene with the gray, fine-tip Pencil tool.

7 Using the Brush tool, color in the large areas of the landscape. Draw in the shapes of the large trees and bushes, but leave the building unpainted.

8 Reduce the Brush tool's tip size (the Pen tool can be used if needed). Draw main shadows, highlights, and smaller foliage. Use the Water Drop tool to soften shadows.

9   Color the building, using the Pen and/or Brush tool. Pay attention to how light hits the structure. Some areas may need to be shadowed. At this point, save your work; it's a finished piece.

10   Do a Save As and rename your art. In this step, you will see one of the great advantages of computer art: the ability to change things very quickly and simply. In this case, we will take the saved piece, which has an opaque style, and turn it into a more transparent wash style. Select the Water Drop tool and lightly blend the colors in the sky. Do you notice how you can pull one color into another or blend the two together? Delicately smudge and blend the hills, trees, and ground. Background areas should be smudged more than the foreground. The building and road only need the slightest smudging, as you don't want to lose too much of their detail.

IMPRESSIONISTIC LANDSCAPE

Nature's details and colors lend themselves perfectly to the impressionistic style of painting. Pick a garden scene with a person in the foreground and trees in the background. Trees make a nice backdrop of shapes and colors. Using the gray Pencil tool, draw in the main pieces of your scene.

11 Using a small tip on the Brush tool, apply dabs of color on the background. Layer the colors onto one another, concentrating on color, light, and shadow. Refer to the image in Sample 12.

12 Apply dabs of color to the middle section of your artwork. Leave small integral areas until later.

13 Start applying color to the largest areas of your figure. Switch to the small-tip Pen tool and fill in smaller areas with short strokes and dabs.

14 Add smaller dabs throughout the artwork to give shapes more definition and detail. Change the direction and size of the strokes, giving the feel of varying textures, as seen in the path and fabric in Sample 15. Add variations of blues and purples for shadow and oranges and yellows for highlights.

15 With the Water Drop tool, apply very delicate smudges to the background and shadows. This gives the illusion of smeared paint.

Suggestion: Try the same project a second time using the Oil Paint tool impressionistic and Seurat brush styles in the Extra Drawer.

STILL LIFE

Still life displays are quite practical as well as appealing because their content consists of items found around your home, garden, or studio. This project gives users a chance to draw from real life instead of photos. To set up your still life, you need a vase, tablecloth, leaves and/or flowers, and a few pieces of fruit.

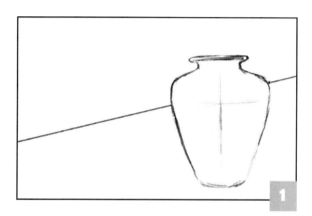

1 Put your still life in view of your computer. When creating your display, use interesting angles because they're more exciting to the eye than a straightforward view. Varying textures, sizes, and colors adds interest to your display. Using the gray Pencil tool, draw the table's edge and the vase. Draw a cross showing the width and height of your vase. The cross becomes a grid, making the proportions of the vase easier to draw, and it is a helpful reference in making the sides equal.

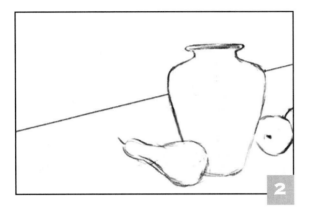

2 Sketch in the shapes of the fruit. With the Eraser tool, erase the overlap lines that cross inside the vase.

3 Using the Pencil tool, draw in the leaves and/or flowers and any decorative details on the table-cloth.

4 Use the Chalk tool, selecting the large tip with your choice of color and an interesting pattern for the background. Lightly draw into the background, leaving some areas white. Refer to Sample 4.

5 Choose a different color and fill in some of the background white areas and partially layer over your previous color.

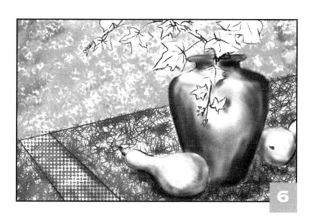

6 Use the Chalk tool and select a pattern for the tablecloth. Fill it in with the chosen color. Use another color and pattern on the trim. Switch to the Spray Paint tool and color in the vase and fruit. Add highlights and shadows. Then switch to the Pen tool and add any needed emphasis lines on the fruit or vase.

7 Using the Chalk and Pen tools, color and detail the leaves and/or flowers. Add stems, obvious veins, highlights, and shadows.

8 Using the Spray Paint tool, apply some dramatic lighting to your artwork. In Sample 8, the display is lit from above and center. The light radiates out, casting shadows underneath and to the right of the objects. Blue-gray shadows cross the left side of the image area. See the finished color image in the Gallery.

Extra Suggestions for Still-Life Subjects: Patterned cloth, baskets, plants, flags, bones, jewelry, cups, bottles, and so on.

SPACE SCENE

Real space travel and fantasy imagery of space as seen in sci-fi movies and the Star Trek series provide exciting reference material that cultivates our imaginations.

1 Select the Graduated Blue to Black Color palette and fill the entire image using the Paint Bucket tool. Next, change to the Stencil tool and select Circle. Using the Spray Paint tool, color in the circle to look like a round sphere. Deselect the Circle Stencil when you're finished. Continue using the Spray Paint tool and put streams of flames coming off the sphere. Change to the Liquid tool and smear a few of the flames. Using the Eraser tool, add a few background stars.

2 Create a planet using the Stencil tool with the Circle selected. Use the gray Chalk tool and a texture to apply to the surface of the planet in the Circle Stencil. Use the Spray Paint and Eraser tools to create larger stars with starbursts and rings around them. Make little sparkles and smaller stars by using the Ink Bottle tool with white selected.

WATER SCENE

Water scenes can be dramatic or serene. The reflective and distortive qualities of water add interest to artwork.

Reference Materials: Collect pictures of boats or water scenes.

1 Stormy Waters

With the Pencil tool, sketch a sailing ship angled up slightly. Break it down into simple shapes. Color the ship using the Ink tool. Create a stormy scene around your ship using the Brush tool. Make waves and swells at different angles. When coloring the water, create areas that are dark, light, and variations of gray, blue, or green.

2 Use the Spray Paint tool to add shadows to the sails and waves. Add a few white highlights with the Ink Bottle tool. Smudge water with the Water Drop and Liquid tools.

3 Using the Spray Paint and Chalk tools, add dramatic shadows to the water. Distort waves slightly with the Liquid tool.

4 **Tranquil Waters**

Use a picture of a pond with lily pads, rocks, and greenery. Use the gray Pencil tool with the fine tip selected to sketch in your image.

5 Use the Spray Paint tool to put in a light undercoating of color. Don't spray white areas.

6 Add more definition to the background, using a small tip on the Spray Paint tool. Add more detail to the shapes using the Pen tool.

7 With the Pen tool and black selected, draw in dark background shapes and silhouettes. Start darkening edges around the pond.

8 Using the Spray Paint, Chalk, and Pen tools, add color and definition to the shapes in the middle- and foreground. Use the Water Drop tool to blend and soften colors and edges. Add emphasis lines to the shadowed edges of lily pads. The Pencil tool can be used for fine lines, as in the grass shown in the foreground in Sample 8.

9 Use the Spray Paint tool to add reflections, shadows, and ripples on the water's surface. Some shadows may extend over the lily pads. In Sample 9, overhanging branches reflect in the water, and shadows are cast from the lily pads. At this point, keep shadows light, so that they don't get overdone. Shadows can be in blues, purples, grays, and dark green.

10 Add texture to rocks. Apply final descriptive detailing to plants, fish, ground, rocks, and so on. Study your work closely to see if there is enough contrast. If there isn't, darken shadows and define shapes that need it. In Sample 10, much of the background contrast was built up. More shadowing was put on and around the rock and the plants around it. A few final highlights were added, using the Eraser tool. See the finished color image in the Gallery.

MASKS

Throughout the world, cultures wear masks in celebrations and ceremonies. Some masks relate to religious beliefs, and other masks are made for fun and holidays. For inspiration, study African, Aztec, Indian, Egyptian, Oriental, Mexican, and other cultures' mask art. Mask colors range from bright colors to earth tones, black and white, pastels, or mixtures of all.

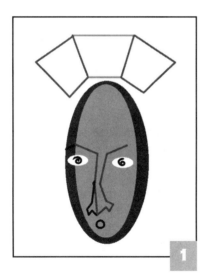

1

1 This project allows the artist a chance to use imagination and to experiment with colors and shapes. Start out with the main shape of any mask. In Sample 1, I used the Stencil tool and the Paint Bucket tool to create a colored oval inside another oval. Add features to your mask's face, using Stencil tool shapes and the Pen tool with Straight Lines selected. Once you've created the face, start adding interesting shapes around it.

2 Use the Pen tool to outline with both the Freehand and Straight Line selections. Design in and around your mask's face.

Apply some of the following:

■ Repeating patterns or lines

■ Geometric shapes and/or symbols

■ Motifs

■ Symmetrical and asymmetrical designs

■ Different sizes of enclosed shapes

3 Using the Paint Bucket tool, fill your shapes with colors. Be careful not to click on the line or the line color will change.

4 Using the Stencil and Paint Bucket tools, create small geometric shapes to embellish your design. Once you create a shape and have it selected, you can Copy and Paste it, move it, and then use the Paint Bucket tool to change the color. This process can be repeated using other shapes.

5 The final decorative element is little white dots. Select the Eraser tool with a fine tip. Lightly click on the mask's surface and draw small dots, which you can group or keep by themselves. Refer to Sample 5. See the finished color image in the Gallery.

SCRATCHBOARD TECHNIQUES

Traditional scratchboard is done with a razor-edged crow quill pen tip in a crow quill holder. Artists scratch a drawing onto special black ink-coated boards.

1 Use a fine-tip Pen tool with white selected and lightly sketch a stylized moon and/or sun with facial features.

2 Draw in only white and highlighted areas. This is the opposite of how you draw on white paper. Using the Pen tool and a fine tip, build up whites, applying cross-hatching and line techniques. Change to the Ink Bottle tool and add stippling effects. Stippling makes great stars, sparkles, and sun rays.

3   Place a potted plant on a pedestal, or find a picture of one. Using the fine-tip Pen tool, with white selected, sketch the basic shapes of the pot and plant. Next, sketch the pedestal. Select Straight Lines to draw in any items with straight lines.

4   Use the Pen tool to add details inside the shapes. Apply cross-hatching and line techniques. Leave shaded areas black. See Sample 4.

5 Apply an interesting border using the Pen tool with Straight Line selected. (Hold down the Shift key to keep lines parallel or vertical.)

6 Add contrast and interest by applying pen technique fills on parts of the border.

CARTOONS

Cartoons can be created in many styles. They can be humorous or political, and their characters can do superhuman feats.

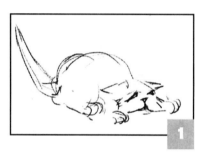

1 Choose to draw either a cat or a dog. Find pictures of them in funny poses. Use the gray Pencil tool to create a sketch of the animal you select. Simplify form and exaggerate features, expressions, and the pose.

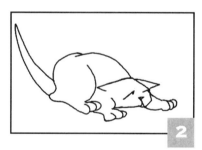

2 Use Tracing Paper to trace over your Pencil tool drawing, and then use the Pen tool with black and fine tip selected to smooth and simplify lines.

3 Add color, using the Pen tool with a medium tip, but leave highlighted areas white. Draw in black shadows and emphasize key lines.

SYMBOLS

Symbols surround us daily. We see symbols on street signs, as trade-marks, on our computers, in artwork, and throughout world cultures.

1 Think of an object or theme that can be made into a symbol. Use only black and white and simple shapes. In Sample 1, I used the Stencil tool with the Heart selected and filled it with black using the Paint Bucket tool. The heart is a symbol for love and the base for my new symbol. Using the Stencil tool, I created a white box and pasted two more into the heart with one running halfway out of the border.

2 With the Polygon Stencil and Paint Bucket tools, I created a black triangle matching the other half of the square. This helped add balance and interest in the interplay of positive and negative spaces.

3 When finalizing your design, make sure the symbol image clearly reflects your concept. In Sample 3, the love theme is reinforced by two adjoining figures. Another black triangle and two squares were added to the design. Finally, two white circles were added, making the combined shapes look like two stylized human figures.

SPECIAL EFFECTS

Technology has brought exciting special effects into the movies.
Dabbler users can create a few of their own special effects.

1   Turn on your Recorder tool. Draw the face of a fearsome animal, having the image fill the page. Refer back to the animal sessions if you'd like.

2   In this step, you make laser beams come out of the animal's eyes. Decide which direction you want the laser beams to go. Then use the Spray Paint tool with a medium-size tip and bright green selected from the Color palette. Using Straight Lines, place a line from one eye to the edge. Press the Enter key and then place a parallel line from the other eye to the edge.

3   Change to the fine-tip size on the Spray Paint tool. Select white from the Color palette. With Straight Lines selected, put a white line down the middle of the green line and bring it back over the line a second time. Press the Enter key and repeat the white line on the other beam.

4   Use the Liquid tool with a small tip and stretch the animal's teeth into longer fangs. Save the new Recorder session and play it back. See the finished color image in the Gallery.

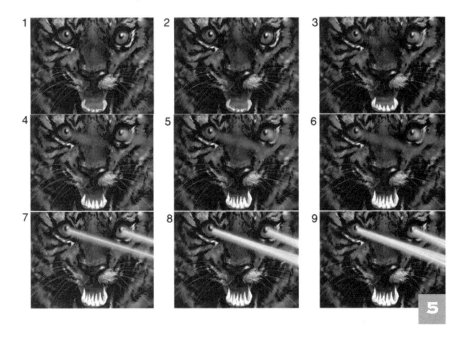

The same project used throughout this session can be made into an animated Flipbook. The Flipbbook lets you elaborate and extend the length of the piece. Play the *Tiger Zap* Flipbook sample included on the Dabbler CD.

To open it, go under the Tutors menu in the **Load Other...** folder, and select *Tiger Zap*. *Tiger Zap* includes other effects that can be applied to the frames. In the sample, the tiger's eyes turn red as the background darkens.

The frames in *Tiger Zap* were created by copying the original tiger illustration onto the first frame of the Flipbook. This illustration was then copied onto the next frame (**Command-A** then **Command-V**). It was then copied to the next frame where slight changes were added (lasers starting to come out of the eyes, the Liquid tool was used to stretch the fangs, etc.).

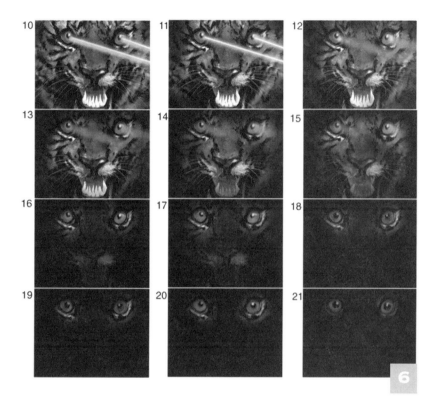

After this, the frames were copied in reverse with the background edges becoming progressively darker. The Spray Paint tool was used to create black shadows. When the progression went back to the first frame image of the tiger, it was copied to the next six frames. On these frames, advancing black shadows grew around the eyes. The eye colors were changed from green, to orange, to red by using the Spray Paint tool.

Use the previous steps to create your own special effects movie. Refer to Chapters 3 and 4 for more information on the Flipbook feature.

FANTASY ART

Dabbler is perfect for creating fantasy subjects with exotic backgrounds. Tools such as the Water Drop, Liquids, Spray Paint, and Chalk with textural effects give the elusion of movement and dream-like qualities.

DRAGONS

Dragons are wonderful subjects because there are limitless combinations of features and appendages that can be used in their creation. They're usually found in caves, around castles, or in forbidden lands. Dragons are active creatures, sometimes flying, swimming, spitting fire, snorting smoke, fighting, or wreaking havoc.

Reference Material: Fairy tales and myths activate and inspire the imagination. Animal books are good reference material for mixing animal parts into the dragon. An example would be drawing a lizard with bat's wings, tiger's claws, and shark's teeth.

1 Think ahead about the pose you want to create. Is it dramatic? Does it show movement and make the dragon look powerful? Begin the drawing with the Pencil tool, making outlines dark so that you can see them later when colors are applied.

2 Consider eventual color choices. Will they show up well? Will they create a special mood? Pick a paper texture that makes the dragon's skin look like scales, fur, etc.

Use the Crayon or Chalk tool to pick up the texture when coloring the dragon's body. Sculpt the body with tints and tones.

3 Change to the Spray Paint tool and paint in wings, sky, and other areas. Enlarge your view, using the Magnifying tool, and add details with the Pencil and Pen tools. Add a cloudy sky as background, using the Spray Paint tool.

4 Darken shadows on underneath areas and apply highlights with the Eraser tool.

With the Spray Paint tool, add wisps of movement trailing off the dragon into the sky. Add a stormy turbulence to the sky, using the Liquid tool. Be careful not to get too close to the dragon's body because the Liquid tool may distort it. From the mouth, draw sprays of fire with the Spray Paint tool.

5 Conclude the drawing with final descriptive details and finishing touches, such as sparkles in the sky made with the Ink Bottle tool and white selected. See the finished image in the Gallery.

PHOTO RETOUCHING AND MANIPULATION

Dabbler's tools work well for creating art from scanned photo images or CDs.

1 If you have a scanner, scan in Sample 1 of the car. If you have CD photo clip art of a car, use that, but crop out the background. Use RGB colors. Save as PhotoShop or other acceptable formats for Dabbler.

2 Use the Spray Paint, Eraser, and Pen tools with white selected to highlight and add definition to the car. Put bright highlights on the bumper, on the top of the fender, and on the hubcap. Add fine-line highlights to the wheel rim and the detailing on the bumper, with the Pen tool and a fine tip. With the Spray Paint and Dropper tools, smooth out any bumps on the car body.

3 Add contrasting black shadows to the car body with the Spray Paint tool. Darken the front of the tire. Still using the Spray Paint tool, add stronger white highlights where the light above would hit the strongest.

4 Use the Pen tool to draw flames on the fender. Use red, yellow, and orange colors with slight highlights of white. With the Liquid tool and a small tip selected, lightly shape and blend flames. Touch up with the Pen tool, using black and white around the flames' edges.

5 Make small flames along the top of the hood, repeating the previous step.

6

6 Use the Stencil tool with Polygon selected to outline the background above the bumper, around the car edge to the image area borders. Switch to the bucket and fill with a blend of your choice from the Graduation palette. With the Water Drop and/or Pen tool, touch up any edges along the car, and blend. Switch to the Dropper tool and select the graduation color just above the left of the bumper. Change to the Spray Paint tool and bring some of that color below the car, fading it into the shadows. See the finished color image in the Gallery.

MULTIPLE IMAGE

1 This project is for users who have a photo-imaging program. In this project you will create a new image and file from a combination of finished session images. Use your dragon, reptile, and one of the following: landscape, water scene, or garden scene (pick the one you think will work best). In your photo program, open Dabbler art after saving it in the appropriate format. Your landscape, water scene, or garden scene will be your new scene, so give it a new name. Open the Dragon Session art, isolate the dragon with the appropriate tool, and resize it to fit in your scene. Copy and paste it into the right position in your selected scene. Repeat this process with the reptile. (It's not necessary to save the altered art after you paste your resized images.) Save the file with a new name in a format Dabbler accepts.

2 Open a new scene in Dabbler. With the Spray Paint and Water Drop tools, blend in edges. Add structures (rocks, branches, etc.) under the reptile and dragon if they are needed. Use the Spray Paint tool to add shadows under the dragon and reptile.

3 Lightly color your lizard, using the Spray Paint tool. Keep color transparent so that original details show. Add some slight texture over the Spray Paint using the Chalk tool with Textures.

Use the Spray Paint tool to add shadow directly onto the lizard and dragon.

4   Put in any color reflections that are needed. In Sample 4, red reflects in the water from the skin of the dragon. Water ripples that would be caused by the movement of the dragon's wings are made with the Spray Paint and Liquid tools.

Using the Spray Paint tool, add streaming sun rays and add highlights where the rays hit.

FLIPBOOK CHARACTER ANIMATION

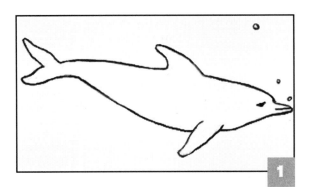

1 In your Sketchpad, draw a simple character with the Pencil tool. Try to use a person, animal, or object with simple lines. Now think of a simple movement for your subject to perform. For example, walking, flying, eating, etc.

Select and copy your character. Create a new Flipbook, and paste your character into the first frame.

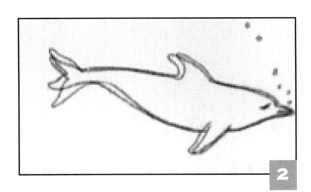

2 Go to the second frame and click on the **Tracing Paper** icon. Trace over the subject with slight changes in movement. Refer to the Dolphin sample.

3 Continue doing Steps 1 and 2 on the next few frames. After every few frames are drawn, play the Flipbook to see how well the movement is working.

Change your **Flipbook Options** tracing layers accordingly (when you want to simultaneously see other frames before and/or after the frame you're working on).

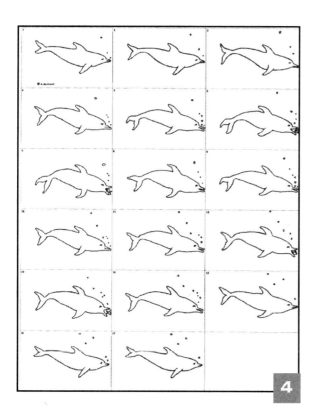

4 When you've completed the last frame, print the Flipbook. Play the Flipbook one last time to be sure the movements work.

EXTENSIONS

RECOMMENDATIONS FOR PERIPHERALS AND SOFTWARE EXTENSIONS

This chapter covers information about customizing your computer worksta-tion. When buying computer equipment and software, a bit of knowledge, research, and comparison shopping really pay off. I've saved a lot of money and eliminated a few headaches by spending a little time researching products.

It's important to decide what type of projects you want to do and in which direction you want to head when setting up your workstation. Are you going to use the computer as a hobby or professionally? Think about your equipment budget. Can you get by with low-end products or do you need better-quality equipment?

When making purchases, consider the following:

▪ Is the manufacturer reputable and does it supply tech support?

▪ Is the product upgradable or will it be in the future?

▪ Will the equipment do what you need it to do?

▪ Is a more expensive product going to be of better quality and will it add essential features?

Software

Dabbler works with major photo-imaging programs such as Photoshop. Dabbler files can be saved in Photoshop format.

Besides working in conjunction with other programs, Dabbler accepts third-party Photoshop-compatible plug-in modules, which give you additional effects and fills. Kai's Power Tools is an excellent example.

The advantages of having a photo-imaging program and plug-in modules are that it expands Dabbler's capabilities.

Pressure-Sensitive Drawing Tablets

To take full advantage of Dabbler's capabilities, I strongly suggest using a pressure-sensitive computer drawing tablet. They provide the user with the ability to trace and a natural feel while doing artwork. Pressure-sensitive lines make the artwork look natural. By applying pressure, you can vary line width, opacity, and the amount of texture that's picked up.

Buying a tablet is much like buying a car. The best way to choose is to see how it feels. Computer expositions usually have major tablet vendors demonstrating and offering discounts. Most of the tablet companies have booths with hands-on stations that allow users to try the tablets.

There are a number of good pressure-sensitive tablet brands on the market. A few suggestions and considerations in buying a tablet for yourself are:

■ Does the vendor supply a warranty, good tech support, and have a good reputation for carrying quality products?

■ Consider tablet size in relation to what you'll be using it for. Small-to-midsize tablets are nice because they can replace your mouse and do not take up a lot of desktop space. Large tablets are good for CAD and architectural rendering.

■ Appraise the feel and workings of the *stylus* (pressure-sensitive pen). Is it cordless? Does it need batteries? Does it feel natural to draw with, and does it work well? Does the weight feel comfortable? Does the stylus have an eraser that works with the new Dabbler pen/erase feature?

 **Eraser is a new feature with Wacom tablets that Fractal is putting in their software.**

Printers

The computer market offers numerous color and black-and-white printers. Printers' prices range from hundreds of dollars to tens of thousands of dollars, depending on their capabilities. Budget and features relating to your project needs are important when choosing a printer.

When purchasing a printer, consider the following:

■ Are the resolution and quality of print adequate for your needs?

■ Does it supply the necessary features and speed?

■ Price per print. Does the printer need a special ribbon, ink, and/or paper?

Prints from Service Bureaus

If you don't have a printer or you need a special type of print, you can take your files to a service bureau. Service bureaus offer a variety of computer output services. Most service bureaus offer laser, color, and high-resolution output.

Scanners

Scanners produce digital imagery from photos and art. These images can be retouched and manipulated in Dabbler and other programs.

There are a variety of scanners available. Some scanners do only black and white, while others scan both black and white and color.

Handheld scanners are an inexpensive way of scanning simple black-and-white images.

Flatbed scanners can scan at high resolutions, giving the user more detailed scans. Black and white or color flatbed scanners are available.

Ask the following questions when buying a scanner:

- Are the quality and resolution what you need?
- Does the manufacturer have a good reputation?
- Are the features and speed adequate for your needs?
- Is the scanner bundled with photo-imaging or other software?

CD-ROM Drives

Users benefit greatly by having a CD-ROM drive. Both internal and external CD-ROM drives are available. Internal are nice because they don't take up desk space, but the advantage of an external drive is that it can be hooked up to different computers.

Some of the benefits of having a CD-ROM drive are

■ Easy access to both photo and clip art images. The market is full of countless images and subjects available on CDs.

■ Kodak Photo CDs allow you to have your photos placed on CD.

■ Many software programs are now available on CD. CDs are easier and faster to load than floppy disks.

■ Educational CDs are great learning tools. They include encyclopedias, interactive children's edutainment programs, software learning programs, books, and more.

RAM, Hard Drive, Back-Up Equipment, and Compression Software

Paint programs use a lot of memory. Dabbler's memory requirements are minimal compared to many paint programs, but if you increase the Sketch Pad resolution and drawing size, the file sizes also increase. This may slow down your machine or not allow you to open Dabbler.

Several solutions for increasing memory size and computer performance are

■ Add more RAM and a larger hard drive to your computer.

■ Store files and large Sketch Pads on a SyQuest, Bernoulli, optical, or some type of backup system.

■ Use file-compression software.

■ RAM Doubler and other RAM expansion programs will increase the RAM capacity of your computer (but may not work with all applications).

Modem and On-Line Services

On-line services and modem sales are growing by leaps and bounds. Because the technology and services are being upgraded daily, I suggest you do current research when you're ready to buy a modem and subscribe to a service.

The advantages of having a modem and on-line service are

■ You have access to limitless amounts of information, including reviews and information about software and computer products.

■ Modems allow users to download files, graphics, images, and multimedia files from on-line services.

■ You can contact vendors directly via on-line services. Fractal Design Corporation has an on-line service and forum that gives information about its products.

■ You can send and receive files from other computer users. Fax/modems are also available, allowing you to transmit documents to fax machines.

Tips on Purchasing Computer Equipment

As previously stated, research is the most important part of choosing computer equipment. The following list provides general tips on choosing and purchasing computer equipment.

■ Ask friends and associates how they like their equipment.

■ Research through magazines, books, reviews, and on-line services.

■ Find out if equipment is upgradable.

■ Be careful when buying second-hand or outdated equipment. Upgrades can be more expensive than if you'd bought new equipment.

■ Are the equipment and software user-friendly or complicated?

■ Take classes or join computer user groups to learn about computer equipment and programs.

■ Computer expositions offer product information and a chance to try products. At these shows, many vendors offer discounts or bundles on software and equipment.

■ Seminars provide opportunities to hear vendors and to network.

■ Compare prices through stores, mail order, user group specials, school discounts, and computer show specials.

AFTER DABBLER

ADVANCING TO PAINTER

After working with the sessions in Section II, you should be functioning fairly well in Dabbler and be fairly knowledgable in the basic principles of art.

At this point, you may want to evaluate your work and feelings toward art. Many of you will probably want to continue exploring and creating artwork in Dabbler. Some of you may want to advance your learning beyond Dabbler's capabilities. Others may want to become professional computer artists.

For those of you wanting more advanced capabilities or commercial work, I suggest advancing to Fractal Design Corporation's Painter program.

Before you buy Painter software, however, there are a couple of considerations to think about: Painter takes more memory to run, and it works better on faster computers.

Painter is a high-end paint program that has endless capabilities. It has become a standard in the computer industry and is used by illustrators, photo retouchers, multimedia artists, animators, designers, special effects artists, and many others.

Painter's interface contains many of the same basic tools and functions as Dabbler. This smooths the transition from Dabbler to Painter. It differs, with many more selections, menu choices, floating palettes, and palette extensions for customizing selections.

Painter does everything you could ever want an art program to do and more. It also works in conjunction with many other programs and plug-in modules. Dabbler files can be brought into Painter and vice versa. I believe an artist could spend his or her whole life using Painter and never be able to use all its customizing capabilities.

Some of the features Painter offers are

- Precision customizing capabilities of Brushes and Art Materials
- Variety of Graduates and Weaves
- Wet Paper and Watercolor Brushes
- Lighting and Textures
- Image Hose (sprays on layers of images)
- Friskets, Masking, and Layering tools
- Animation capabilities

GALLERY

The Gallery features artwork by a variety of Dabbler users and artists. Included are pieces by professionals, amateurs, students, children, and disabled or developmentally disabled adults. The Gallery also provides information about the artists and how they created their Dabbler artwork.

Some of the Session pieces by the author are featured in the color section of the Gallery. Descriptions of these pieces include some helpful information and tips about color usage.

Many of the pieces in the Gallery were created using a higher resolution than the 72 dpi default. High resolution was achieved by creating custom Sketchpads in Dabbler (refer to Section I, Chapter 4: *Advanced Dabbler* for more information). A few Gallery pieces were created in Fractal Design Corporation's Painter program using the same tools found in Dabbler. Enjoy the Gallery art and study the techniques described in this section to improve your Dabbler skills.

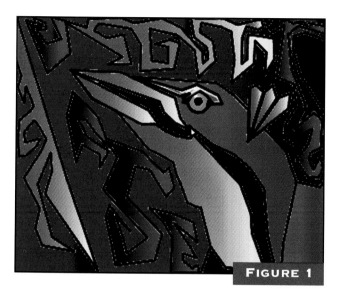

FIGURE 1

BIRD MOTIF

Black lines create an interesting framework for solid and graduated fills. The Paint Bucket tool was used to fill the design. A complementary color scheme of oranges and blues provides a vibrancy to the artwork. Refer to Section II, Session 7 for more information.

FIGURE 2

BUTTERFLY STENCIL COLLAGE

This stencil collage is composed of simple Polygonal and Freehand Stencil tool shapes and solid fills. The combination of colors and shapes pull your eye through the design. The large magenta background shape complements the shades of greens in the leaves. Other colors and white add interest to the piece. Refer to Section II, Session 8 for more information.

FIGURE 3

CACTUS SCENE CREATED WITH BRUSHES

Bold, brilliant colors play against black lines and shapes to create a striking image in this piece. The interplay of the line style, produced with the Brush tool, adds rhythm to the artwork.

The cacti form interesting shapes against the mountains. These shapes are emphasized by using a heavy line for the outer brush strokes. Refer to Section II, Session 12 for more information.

FIGURE 4

FISH

Fish are fun subjects that come in many shapes, colors, and sizes. The dramatic presence of this fish is achieved with the positive and negative (black and white) shapes on its body, in conjunction with the orange, which is complemented by the blue of the water. The yellow highlights are accentuated by using its complementary color, purple, in the shadows.

Transparent layering was applied with the Spray Paint tool, and texture was added with the Chalk tool along with texture from the Texture drawer. Refer to Section II, Session 18 for more information.

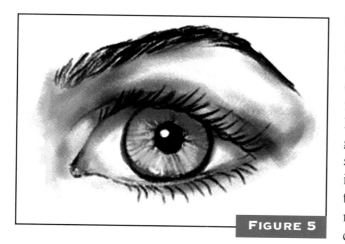

FIGURE 5

EYE

Subtle coloring in combination with fine details give the eye a realistic quality. Retinas can vary greatly in different subjects, so it's important to study the colors and outer rings closely before drawing.

Soft buildup of color on the eye, lid, and shadows, is achieved with the Spray Paint tool. Fine line details in the lashes and eyebrows are drawn with a dark gray/black, small tip Pencil tool. A white highlight in the pupil is created with the fine-tipped Eraser tool. Refer to Section II, Session 15 for more information.

FIGURE 6

PORTRAIT OF A WOMAN

Colors add drama, stylization and luminosity to a portrait. Skin and hair tones can be created with a variety of colors. In this portrait of a woman, several shades of purple were added to her hair. Orange, yellow, and green were added to her skin tone. The shadow is drawn in purple. Refer to Section II, Session 15 for more information.

FIGURE 7

BLUE VASE STILL LIFE

Still life studies teach the artist about form, texture, and lighting. In creating the Blue Vase still life, I took advantage of the textures in Dabbler.

Using the Chalk tool, colors and textures were layered on top of one another, in both the background and on the tablecloth. In contrast with these textures is the smooth, blue reflective surface of the vase. Dramatic lighting was applied with the Spray Paint tool. Refer to Section II, Session 21 for more information.

FIGURE 8

TRUMPET FLOWERS

Flowers are beautiful subjects, and they come in a vast array of shapes and colors. The colors on the flowers were applied with the Spray Paint tool. Soft buildup formed the shape and shadow of the subject. Details were added with the Pen, Chalk and Pencil tools. The Eraser tool was used to create highlights, and the Water Drop tool was used for softening and blending. Refer to Section II, Session 17 for more information about flowers and plants.

FIGURE 9

ALASKAN LANDSCAPE

Dabbler's ability to emulate traditional mediums makes it a great program for drawing landscapes. To create the Alaskan Landscape, the Chalk, Pen, Spray Paint, Brush, and other tools were used. The Water Drop tool was used for blending, and for making the mountains fade into the distance. The landscape is made up of vibrant colors, earth tones, and pastels. Refer to Section II, Session 20 for more information.

FIGURE 10

LILY POND

Water holds a fascination for most people because of its reflective and distortive qualities. In the *Lily Pond*, the water gives the scene a serene quality. The smooth texture, reflections, and highlights play nicely against the dark shapes and textures of the background and foreground. The orange of the Koi adds interest to the piece. Refer to Section II, Session 23 for more information.

FIGURE 11

DRAGON

Dragons challenge an artist's imagination. Dramatic movement, color, and shadows add to the fantasy appeal of these creatures. Vivid colors combined with exciting textures give this piece its dynamic feel.

The Spray Can tool was used to add sparkles, fire from the mouth, and wisps of movement. These effects add a sense of excitement to the dragon. Refer to Section II, Session 29 for more information.

FIGURE 12

MASK

Simple shapes and decorative elements are the basis of this mask. The Pen tool was used to create the black outlines of the shapes. These shapes were then filled with a variety of hues and tints using the Paint Bucket tool. White dots created with the Eraser tool embellish the mask's surface. Refer to Section II, Session 24 for more information.

FIGURE 13

ONE BAD TIGER

The tiger illustration was created with the Spray Paint, Pencil, Ink Pen, Ink Bottle, and Chalk tools. Laser beams were applied with the Spray Paint tool, using a medium tip for the green, and a small tip for the white. The fangs were stretched with the Liquid tool.

By recording the session, you can play back your steps, emulating special effects with the movement of the laser beams and fangs. Refer to Section II, Session 28 for more information.

FIGURE 14

COOL MERCURY

The *Cool Mercury* art was created from a scan. The Spray Paint tool was used to touch up the car body and chrome parts. Highlights were added using the Ink Pen and Eraser tools. The flames adorning the hood and bumper were drawn with the Ink Pen tool. The Liquid tool was used to stretch the flames. The graduated blue-to-black background was a fill applied with the Stencil and Bucket tools. Refer to Section II, Session 30, for more information.

FIGURE 15

PITCHER

A simple line drawing was scanned and then opened in Dabbler. Colors were applied with the Ink Pen, Chalk, and Spray Paint tools. The Water Drop tool was used for blending and smudging colors, as seen on the grass and fabric. Details in the face were added with the Ink Pen and Pencil tools. Using purple shadows added more interest than using black shadows. Refer to Section II, Session 11 for more information about figure drawing.

FIGURE 16

LADY BY THE SHORE

The figure and background in this image has been stylized. The swirls in the skirt are repeated in the background shapes, emphasizing the idea of wind and waves.

Graduated and solid fills form design shapes that add excitement and movement throughout the image. Black lines, created with the Pen tool, outline and detail the figure. The bird in the background helps balance the image. Refer to Section II, Session 14 for more information on figure drawing, and to Sessions 7 and 8 for information on fills.

FIGURE 17

WOMEN
WENDY MORRIS

Wendy Morris is a jeweler, fine artist, and teacher. Her work is featured in a greeting card line and a children's book. Wendy recently started working on computers. She found Dabbler easy to use and an inspiration to create illustrations on the computer.

To create *Women*, artwork was scanned from an ink drawing. Lines were added using the Ink Pen tool with **Straight Lines** selected. The Paint Bucket tool was used to color the image and add graduated fills.

DANCING CATS
SUZANNE WEBER PARKER

Suzanne Weber Parker has been working as an artist in San Diego since 1976, as an illustrator designer and art director for ad agencies, marketing firms, and the giftware industry as well as her own freelance business, *Weber Art*.

FIGURE 18

To create *Dancing Cats*, Suzanne scanned line art drawn on tracing paper. The image was colored using the Chalk and Spray Paint tools. The Water tool was used for blending, the Pen tool for emphasizing lines, and Eraser tool to create the heart design in the background.

FIGURE 19

MUSEUM OF MAN
DAVID LOCK HIGGINS

David Lock Higgins, who resides in San Diego, is an internationally collected portrait artist. He has been a professional artist, illustrator, and graphic designer for over 40 years. Historically, his artwork has been created in gouache, oils pastels, and oils. David finds that the Macintosh as a painting medium offers him greater expression of form, design, and color than traditional material.

Museum of Man, was inspired by the amazing structure that stands in Balboa Park, San Diego, California. The piece was quickly done using the Cotton Paper texture, and the Pen and Pastel tools. Colors were used from a pre-formatted palette.

FIGURE 20

AH, YOUTH

Ah, Youth is a piece from David's people on the street series. This young person was playing on an escalator, spotted David, and gave him the smile that inspired this drawing.

It was created on the Cotton Paper texture using the Pen tool. This piece shows that every part of a drawing need not be detailed and finished.

SUMANTRAN TIGER

FIGURE 21

Sumantran Tiger by David Lock Higgins was inspired by a beautiful tiger at the San Diego Animal Park. David sketched the major shapes using the Pen tool. He then splattered the surface with the Ink Bottle tool, using vibrant colors. He completed the background with fills using the Paint Bucket tool, and details with the Chalk and Pen tools.

YOUNG FACE

FIGURE 22

Young Face from David Lock Higgins is a portrait study created by using Dabbler's Chalk tool. The flesh tones and pinks on the face combine nicely with the yellow highlights, giving the image a soft warm glow. The red of the shirt adds a nice contrast to the softer colors.

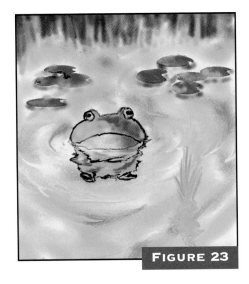

FIGURE 23

FROG IN THE POND
DAVID SANCHEZ

As I watched David Sanchez, age nine, work on the computer, I realized that this was one very talented nine-year-old. When I explained tool usage and techniques, he would apply them perfectly to his work.

David used the Spray Paint, Ink and the Paint Bucket tool to create the *Frog in the Pond* piece. The Liquid tool was used to create the ripples in the water.

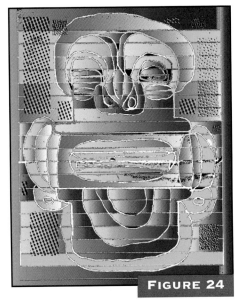

FIGURE 24

FROGMAN
PHILIP CONLON

Philip is a developmentally disabled artist who also has some physical disabilities. Philip has developed his own style of colorful motif painting that is gaining him recognition in shows, publications, and the sale of reproductions. He is inspired by aboriginal peoples' art.

Phil creates art from his imagination, or uses his own interpretations from real-life objects and photos. He says, "I has images in my head and must draw them."

Frogman was scanned from one of Phil's pencil sketches done on lined paper. The lines from the paper add a rhythmic quality to the piece. Paint Bucket fills were the basis of the work. Surface Textures were applied in stenciled areas. The Negative tool was used on the whole image.

FIGURE 25

HORNED MASK

Phils style lends itself nicely to the computer as seen in *Horned Mask*. The mask image was drawn using the Ink tool. The Paint Bucket tool was used to fill the enclosed shapes. The black filled areas and lines, with Phil's choice of vivid colors, create a visual treat.

FIGURE 26

Phil Conlon's textured mask image was created from a scanned pencil drawing. Fills were created using the Bucket tool. Textures were drawn using the Chalk tool with several textures.

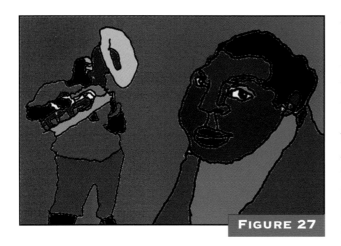

FIGURE 27

JAZZ
MARK RIMLAND

Mark Rimland is an autistic savant artist. Mark has a national reputation for his artwork. He is a skilled artist in both traditional mediums and the computer. His style has a very sensitive line quality with a contour drawing feel to it.

Jazz showcases Marks wonderful line work. The lines were drawn with the Pencil and Ink tools. Fills were added using the Paint Bucket tool. The red and black color scheme add richness to the mood, while the light blue used in the face forms a focal point.

FIGURE 28

This smiling profile by Mark has a poster-style quality. The drawing was done with the Pencil and Ink tools. Graduated and solid fills were applied with the Paint Bucket. Mark used the base drawing to create several versions of this piece.

FIGURE 29

VILLAGE
KRISTINA WOODRUFF

Kristina is a talented autistic savant, living in San Diego, who's winning national acclaim for her artwork. Kristina's art shows a great sense of color and line control, creating a special quality of drama and mood. Buildings, people, and animals are a few of the subjects that inspire her.

Bay Front Village was one of Kristina's simple pencil sketch drawings scanned and then drawn over in Dabbler. Lines were sketched in with the Pencil and Ink tools, and colorful fills were added.

FIGURE 30

WHALES

Kristina's *Whales* were drawn with the Ink, Chalk, and Spray Paint tools. She then added whites with the Eraser tool. The mixture of tools give the effect of water and movement.

FIGURE 31

SIDE SHOW
CHRISTOPHER KAESER

Christopher Kaeser is a graduate of the Ringling School of Art and Design, currently practicing illustration.

Side Show was created using the Chalk tool upon an initial Pencil tool drawing. Layered strokes were applied from dark to light. The Pen tool was used for highlighting areas.

FIGURE 32

COURTNEY BRUNER

Courtney Bruner, a student at Ringling School of Art and Design, Sarasota, Florida, dedicated her piece to computer artists. She used random Brush tools to create the background colors. The Liquid tool was used swirled to colors. The face, hand, and stylus were created with the Chalk and Ink tools. The Water Drop tool was used to blend these images.

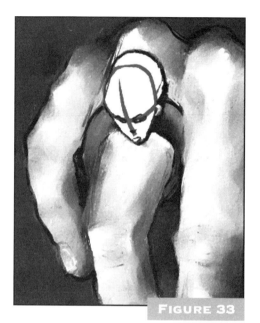

FIGURE 33

RINGMAN

Ringman by Courtney, was created with the Ink and Chalk tools. Soft blending was achieved with the Water Drop tool. The head on the ring was left white as a focal point.

FIGURE 34

DANCERS

Courtney used loose lines and ellipses to create *Dancers*. The tools used were the Ink Pen for the figures and stars, and the Paint Bucket for the background fill. The Water Drop tool was used for blending the area around the dancers.

SELF PORTRAIT

Self Portrait by Courtney Bruner was inspired by her reflection on the monitor. Reflective portraits are novel projects.

FIGURE 35

Courtney's portrait was done with the Ink, Chalk, and Water Drop tools over a black background. The white dots in the background were created with the white Chalk tool and the Basketball texture. The Liquid tool was used to swirl the dots.

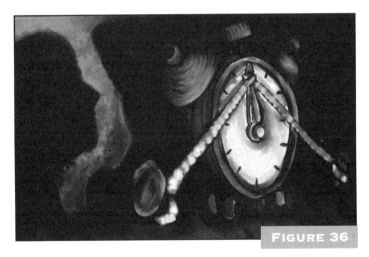

CLOCK

Clock by Courtney Bruner was created with the Ink, Chalk, and Water Drop tools. The silhouette's negative shapes add drama to the piece.

FIGURE 36

FIGURE 37

CHRISTOPHER KAESER

MODEL

The artwork, *Model,* was a Dabbler pencil drawing. The inspiration for the image was a sketch from Chris's sketchbook at a life-drawing class. Chris found Dabbler's Pencil tool to be perfect for creating simple sketches.

OLD MAN

FIGURE 38

Old Man by Christopher Kaeser was created by using layers of the Chalk and Spray Paint tools applied over a Paint Bucket filled background. A Glass Distortion focus was applied in a stencil around the head. The Water Drop tool was used for blending.

FIGURE 39

DAVID LOCKE HIGGINS

MY FAVORITE THINGS

David's piece, entitled *My Favorite Things*, shows how well Dabbler's tools work for creating realistic artwork. The Water Drop tool allows the artist to do soft controlled blending.

The Eraser creates wonderful highlights, giving the artist choices of transparency selections in the Extras Drawer.

FIGURE 40

RED HAT FOR 4TH OF JULY

Red Hat for 4th of July is part of David's people of the street series. It was done on Cotton paper texture using various sizes of the Chalk tool. David finds the basic tools in Dabbler allow for looseness and spontaneity. He also feels his pressure-sensitive drawing tablet is a key accessory in working with Dabbler and other art programs.

FIGURE 41

JEREMY SUTTON

Jeremy is an internationally recognized digital artist. He demonstrates at many of the major computer trade shows and is currently a faculty member of the Academy of Art College in San Francisco and San Francisco State University.

Eagle was created using a variety of drawing and painting tools, and the Liquid tool applied over them. The highlight in the eye was applied with the Eraser tool.

FIGURE 42

HARPS OF WORLD

Harps of World abstract was done with a variety of drawing and painting tools. Distortion effects were created with the Liquid tool.

FIGURE 43

RAY BLAVATT

Ray Blavatt is the animator and illustrator for Conexus, a San Diego company that creates interactive educational CD ROMs for children.

In addition to working at Conexus, Ray demonstrates pressure-sensitive drawing tablets for Wacom at MacWorld, SIGGraph, Seybold, and other computer exhibitions.

The cartoon of the man with a mustache was drawn with the Pencil, Chalk, and Water Drop tools.

FIGURE 44

SUPER HERO

Super Hero was created with the Pencil and Spray Paint tools. The Water Drop tool was used for blending shadows.

FIGURE 45

BASEBALL DREAMS

Baseball Dreams is a simple Pencil tool cartoon sketch. This drawing illustrates how well Dabbler's Pencil tool emulates a real pencil.

FIGURE 46

BLAZING TRAILS

Blazing Trails was created with the Pencil and Spray Paint tools. The Water Drop tool was use to do soft smudging.

FIGURE 47

BETH SHIPPER

Beth is a resident artist in San Diego. Her work includes over 20 years of illustration, cartooning, designing, and writing. She is skilled in both traditional and computer art. She loves working on children's educational software.

Snow Bird was created with Pencil and Spray Paint tools. The Eraser tool was used to add highlights.

FIGURE 48

CABOOSE AND CABOOLE

Beth's *Caboose and Caboole*, is a illustration from a cookbook for the Poway Midland Railroad Volunteers of Poway. This illustration began with a Pencil tool sketch. Textures were used in the grass. Spray Paint color was added.

FIGURE 49

TAD SHELBY

Tad Shelby is Product Manager for Fractal Design Corporation. One of his favorite effects in Dabbler is the Fade effect, because it lets an artist create transparent Stencil layers.

In creating the fish image, Tad first laid down a background using the Spray Paint tool. The fish was made with a Stencil from the Stencil Library. The seaweed was created with the Freehand Stencil, Bucket fills, and the Fade effect.

FIGURE 50

ELENA SMITH PELAYO

Elena began working on computers many years ago as a typesetter. She demonstrates pressure-sensitive tablets and art software. She is currently editor of *Macintouch*, the monthly publication of the San Diego Mac User Group.

Waiting for Love was drawn with the Pen tool. The Chalk tool was used to add a variety of textures, along with the **Impressionist** Oil Paint tool and the Spray Paint tool. The Water Drop tool was used for smudging.

JANE NEWCOMB

IRISES

Jane is a fine artist and graphic design-er. She also instructs art retreats. Jane is inspired by Dabbler's tools and user-friendly interface.

FIGURE 51

Irises was created using a Wacom tablet. Jane used the Pencil, Spray Paint, and Chalk tools. The final step was blending the image with the Water Drop tool.

KATHLEEN BLAVATT

Among the Lily Pads by *Dabbler* author Kathleen Blavatt. The water was drawn with the **Seurat** Oil Paint tool. The Liquid tool was applied to give a rippled effect.

FIGURE 52

The Chalk, Spray Paint, and Water Drop tools were used on the face, hand, and lilies. The Liquid tool was used to give the hair a wet look, stretching the strands of hair into the flow of the water. Glimmers were added with the **Seurat** Oil Paint tool with white selected. Then the Spray Paint tool shadows were applied.

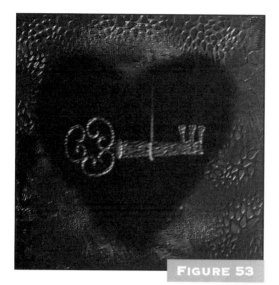

FIGURE 53

JENNIFER HANSEN

Jennifer is a computer illustrator from San Diego, California, and an Art Center Graduate.

Key & Heart was created using the large Chalk tool with texture background "artbeats" and the "trees and leaves" paper palettes. Then surface texture was applied.

The heart was drawn with the Chalk tool. The key was painted with the Chalk tool and Paper Texture palette. The surface texture was applied again. The string was drawn with the Chalk tool.

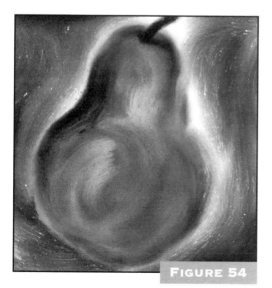

FIGURE 54

PEAR

Jennifer's *Pear* used the large Chalk tool to draw the entire image. Several Paper Textures were used.

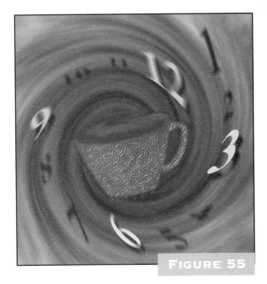

FIGURE 55

COFFEE FUNNEL

Coffee Funnel was created using the large Chalk tool to paint the background. The funnel was created by selecting the background and applying the "twirl" filter from Photoshop. Using the Rotation tool, the canvas was turned at different angles while the numbers were typed in individually. The Motion Blur effect was then applied individually. The cup was drawn with the Chalk tool over texture, and Freehand tool outline was used with Texture effect.

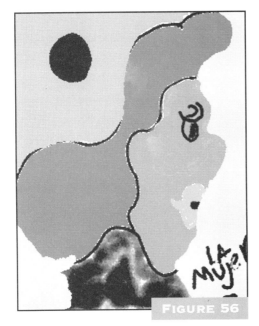

FIGURE 56

ANGELA BOYCE

Angela Boyce is a history major attending the University of California. She has been working on computers since the age of four. She started on a Commodore computer and currently works on a Macintosh Powerbook. Drawing and poetry are Angela's hobbies. She enjoys creating cartoon caricatures on the computer for her friends.

Angela's whimsical drawing, *La Mujer*, was created with the Ink Pen tool, Paint Bucket fills, and the Spray Paint tool.

FIGURE 57

MITCH

Angela's portraits have a child-like quality, yet are sophisticated in the way she captures a person's appearance and personality with minimal lines and color. The portrait of *Mitch* emphasizes his accessories, in turn emphasizing his personality.

FIGURE 58

FRANK

The portrait of *Frank* by Angela was drawn on computer at an art opening. The Ink tool and Paint Bucket fills used in the drawing caught Frank's personality wonderfully.

FIGURE 59

KRISTINA WOODRUFF

APARTMENTS

Kristina is an autistic savant artist who has been creating computer art since 1991. Her favorite programs are Dabbler, Painter, and FreeHand. Her artwork has been exhibited at many computer shows. Kristina attends art classes at St. Madeleine Sophie's Center and takes private lesson with Kathleen Blavatt.

Kristina's *Apartments* was drawn with the Pencil, Ink, and Chalk tools. The **Straight Line** option was selected during the drawing stages. The Paint Bucket tool was used to apply graduated fills.

FIGURE 60

TAOS

Kristina's *Taos* piece demonstrates her ability to draw buildings. It was drawn freehand using the Pencil, Ink, and Chalk tools. The Spray Paint tool was used to paint the sky.

FIGURE 61

BALBOA PARK

Balboa Park by Kristina again showcases her skill at drawing buildings. This image was drawn using the Pencil tool.

FIGURE 62

KREMLIN

Kristina loves drawing Russian buildings. She's painted several versions of the Kremlin and this is the first one she created on computer. In this piece, she's created her own color scheme and emphasized the patterns on the onion domes. The tools used were Ink, Spray Paint, and Chalk.

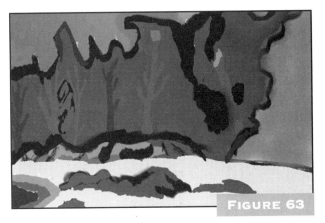

FIGURE 63

TREES ALONG THE SHORELINE

Kristina's *Trees Along the Shoreline* was drawn in a style emphasizing flat color shapes with some strong outlines. The artwork was created with Pencil, Ink, Brush, and Chalk tools.

FIGURE 64

THE NUTCRACKER

A favorite holiday subject of Kristina's is the nutcracker. This nutcracker illustrates Kristina's quick, loose style of drawing. *The Nutcracker* was drawn with the Pencil tool.

FIGURE 65

This drawing was inspired by an old silent movie photo. The photo was black and white, but Kristina uses a vast array of colors in her artwork. The piece was created with the Pencil, Ink, Spray Paint, and Chalk tools.

FIGURE 66

LION

After seeing the movie *Lion King*, Kristina started drawing a series of wonderful lions from her imagination. This smiling lion was created with the Chalk, Spray Paint, and Water Drop tools.

FIGURE 67

In this desert land-
scape, Kristina uses
her solid, flat color
style of painting.
The Chalk and Spray
Paint tools were the
main ones used. The
Eraser tool was used
to go back into the
work to add white
areas and high-
lights.

SHAMAN MASK

Shaman Mask dis-
plays Kristina's won-
derful use of lines.
This piece was
drawn with the
Pencil and Ink tools.
The Paint Bucket
tool was use to apply
both solid and grad-
uated fills.

FIGURE 68

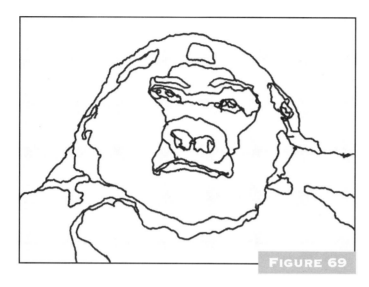

FIGURE 69

MARK RIMLAND

GUERRILLA

Autistic savant artist Mark Rimland has been a featured artist in many publications. His computer art has appeared in many exhibitions, and is reproduced in cards and prints.

Mark's father is Dr. Bernard Rimland, an international autism authority, the founder of the Autism Research Institute in San Diego, and acted as consultant for the movie *Rainman*.

Guerrilla was drawn using the Pencil tool.

FIGURE 70

MOUNTAIN LIONS

Mark's *Mountain Lions* were drawn with the Pencil and Pen tools. Fills were applied with the Paint Bucket tool.

FIGURE 71

CHICKS

Chicks was drawn with the Pen and Chalk tools. Simple black lines form the terrain in the background.

FIGURE 72

ROOSTER

Rooster was drawn with the Pencil, Pen, and Marker tools. The Chalk tool was used with textures on the rooster and ground.

FIGURE 73

THREE BIRDS

Mark created *Three Birds* with the Pencil, Spray Can, Ink, and Chalk tools. The Water Drop tool was used for soft blending. The Eraser was used to add highlights in the birds eyes.

FIGURE 74

WALLABY

The *Wallaby* was sketched with the Pencil tool. The Chalk tool, in different earthtones, was used to create the fur of the animal. The eyes were filled in with the Pen tool, and highlights were added with the Eraser tool.

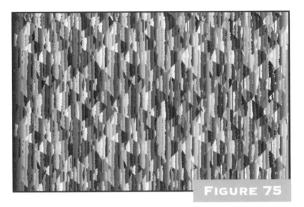

FIGURE 75

DEBORAH GILE

Deborah is deaf and learning impaired, yet in some areas, she is brilliant. Her memory skills on subjects that interest her are incredible. For example, in her art class at St. Madeleine Sophie's Center, she created a drawing of the universe and labeled all the planets and galaxies.

Deborah's passion for computers is all-consuming. She creates fascinating, intricate textural design images of layered shapes and graduated fills. Deborah is a prime example of a handicapped person who has benefited greatly from the addition of computers to her life.

In the image above, she applied a graduated fill to the whole background. Then, still using the Paint Bucket tool, she applied many fills onto the graduated background, creating patterns.

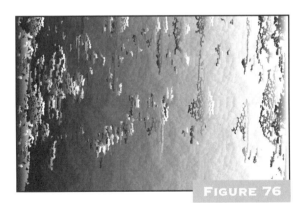

FIGURE 76

In this image as in the previous one, Deborah applied Paint Bucket fills over a graduated fill background. This piece shows how negative and positive space help balance a piece. (As seen in this piece, a graduated fill background will only let you fill small areas creating random shapes, not unlike a solid fill that replaces the whole fill with a new color.)

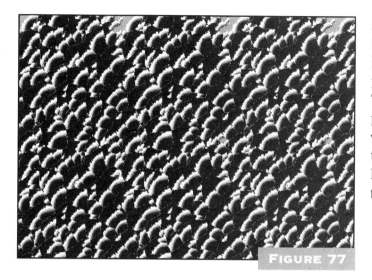

FIGURE 77

Many of Deborah's pieces have a textile or pattern quality. This feather-like pattern image was done using textures and Paint Bucket fills.

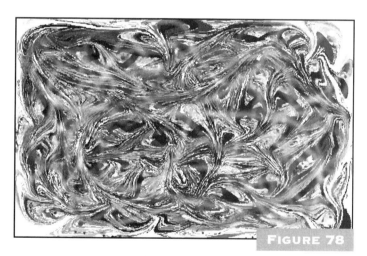

FIGURE 78

This abstract image was Deborah's way of learning the program. She tried most of the Drawing and Painting tools, in many colors, layering them over one another to create this piece.

FIGURE 79

PHIL CONLON
MYSTIC MASK

A quote taken from the *San Diego Union Tribune* describing Philip's artwork states: "The mask drawings of Phil Conlon show a highly developed sense of color and an Aztec or Mayan influence acquired not by direct learning but drawn solely from the subconscious." *Mystic Mask* was scanned from one of Phil's marker sketches. The enclosed shapes were filled with solid colors using the Paint Bucket tool. The magenta line was created by clicking on the line with the Paint Bucket tool and selecting magenta.

LINED MASK

Lined Mask was scanned from one of Phil's pencil sketches on lined paper. The lines add an element of interest to the piece. The enclosed shapes were filled using the Paint Bucket tool with graduated palettes.

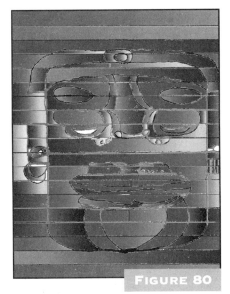

FIGURE 80

Alex Pelayo, age eleven, is the kind of individual who puts great thought into what he does. Alex wants to makes a statement through his art.

FIGURE 81

This first piece Alex created is an anti-drug illustration in which he created several versions of the same image using different filters.

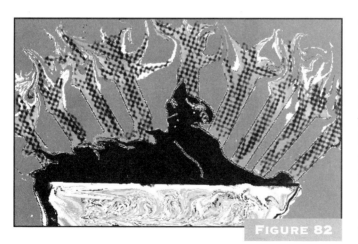

The pieces Alex creates have a very dramatic feel to them as seen in this fiery panther work. In creating this piece, Alex used a variety of textures with the Chalk tool. He used the Liquid Brush tool to distort his image.

FIGURE 82

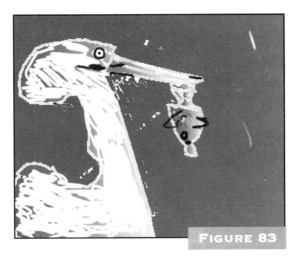

FIGURE 83

DAVY McCOLLOCH

STORK

I met Davy and his mother through Macintosh User Group meetings. Davy was age six the first time he came to my studio. We shared several computer tips and tricks with one another. Davy wants to know everything about computers.

He found Dabbler easy to use, and has been asking his mother to buy the program and a pressure-sensitive tablet.

Stork was created with the Ink tool and Paint Bucket fills. Davy used the Eraser tool to add white to the stork's body.

FIGURE 84

STARMAN

Davy's art shows great imagination, experimentation, and whimsy, as seen in the *Starman* image. Davy experimented with many of the drawing tools in creating *Starman*. He used the Stencil tool to create the stars.

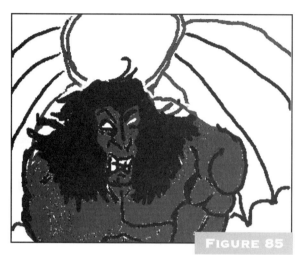

FIGURE 85

DAVID SANCHEZ

BAT WING MAN

David Sanchez, age nine, has been around computers most of his life. His father, Piet Sanchez, runs the San Diego Macintosh User Group, Art and Hypercard SIG (Special Interest Group). David is seen at many of the monthly meetings helping his father.

Dabbler allowed this talented young artist to create wonderful art on the computer. The *Bat Wing Man* was his first attempt on Dabbler. The Ink tool was use to create the image.

FIGURE 86

SHARLENE ANDERSON

Japanese style comic figures are this teen's favorite subject to draw. Sharlene used a variety of tools in creating her artwork. She especially enjoyed using the Liquid tool on the background and the character's top.

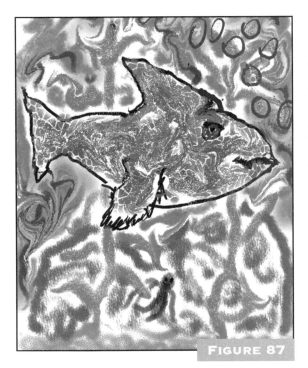

FIGURE 87

FRANCESCA LOMBARDO

The humorous fish, created by nine-year-old Francesca Lombardo, shows the fun children have trying the many Paint and Brush tools in Dabbler. This piece was also an exercise in texture and color.

FIGURE 88

MAX SHAFFER

I knew Max liked to draw early on when, at age two-and-a-half, he surprised his mother and me with a crayon drawing on the front of their refrigerator.

Now eight years old, Max is advancing to computer art using Dabbler. His fish was created with the Pen, Spray Paint, and Crayon tools. The bubbles were created with the large tip Ink Bottle tool (**Leaky Pen** selection).

FIGURE 89

KATIE BARNS

SUNSET

Katie is a twelve-year-old who loves computers. Going on-line is one of her favorite pasttimes. *Sunset* was created with the Pen tool and Paint Bucket fills. The Liquid tool was used to add the design in the water.

FIGURE 90

LOGAN DERRY

Logan, age six, is the daughter of John Derry, a staff artist for Fractal Design Corporation.

Logan's self portrait was created with Dabbler's Drawing and Painting tools, inside a Heart stencil.

FIGURE 91

RUSS FAGALY

Russ is a twelve-year-old computer whiz kid. He and his father beta test and write reviews on software programs. Russ has also won an award for a freeware disk he created, that supplies users with a variety of folder icons (including a Dabbler folder icon). These icons were created with ResEdit and are sold through SDMUG and *Macintouch*. The tiger drawing was created with the Chalk and Water Drop tools.

FIGURE 92

This lizard was drawn with the Chalk tool. The Lizard paper texture was used to create the pattern on the surface of the animal.

Abstract   An unrealistic representation of an image or form.

Animation   The simulation of movement produced by displaying a series of images, objects, or characters.

Application

A computer program to help users perform a specific type of task, such as spreadsheet, database, desktop publishing, word processing, or graphics programs.

Asymmetrical

The unbalanced proportion of forms on opposite sides of the center vertical axis in an image.

Bézier Curve

A curve that is mathematically calculated to connect separate points in smooth, free-form curves and surfaces.

BMP

Bit-mapped files; this file format stores a group of bits that describe the characteristics of individual pixels that make up an image.

Brightness

Part of the HSB (Hue-Saturation-Brightness) color model; brightness is the amount of white (from 0% to 100%) in a color.

CD-ROM

Compact Disc Read-Only Memory; a high-capacity (approximately 600 megabytes) form of computer storage that uses laser optics to read data.

Clip Art

A collection of photographs, diagrams, maps, drawings, and other graphic images that can be "clipped" from the collection and imported into other documents.

Clipboard

A memory resource in operating systems that stores a copy of the last information that was "copied" or "cut"; the information on the Clipboard can be "pasted" into another document.

Clone

A duplicated image that can be manipulated without effecting the original.

CMYK

Cyan, Magenta, Yellow, Black; a method of describing process colors used to prepare an image for print.

Collage

A collection of images, shapes, or pieces used to form one piece.

Color Model

Any method for representing color in desktop publishing and graphic arts, such as HSB, CMYK, and RGB.

Cropping

Cutting off part of an image, such as unneeded sections of a graphic or extra space around borders.

Cross-hatching

A method of shading with strokes that cross one another.

Default

A choice made by a software program when a user does not specify an alternative.

Dialog Box

A window displayed on screen to present choices to a user for specific settings or functions.

DPI

Dots per inch; a measure of screen and printer resolution expressed in terms of how many dots can be displayed or printed per inch.

EPS

Encapsulated PostScript; an independent PostScript file format that can be placed/imported into an application file.

Flipbook

A series of frames used to simulate character movement for animation.

Font

A set of characters of the same typeface, style, stroke weight, and size.

Frame

A single image that can be displayed in a sequence with other, slightly different, images to create animation.

Grayscale	A progressive series of shades ranging from black to white.
Hot Spot	The area of a picture where the light hits most intensely.
HSB	Hue-Saturation-Brightness; a color model used to describe color in computer graphics.
Hue	Part of the HSB (Hue-Saturation-Brightness) color model; hue is the pure color as it appears on the color wheel.
Impressionistic	A type of brush stroke applied to focus on color and light rather than detail.
Inbetweening	The frames used to connect detailed character/image movements in between keyframes.
Intensity	The brightness or dullness of a color.
Intermediate Colors	A primary color mixed with a secondary color.
JPEG	Format used by IBM and compatibles to compress graphics files.
Keyframe	The main frames of character/image movement used as the basis for an animated sequence.
Life Drawing	A type of drawing that focuses on the human figure in various life poses.
Object-Oriented	Graphics that are based on lines, curves, circles, and squares.
Opaque	Nontransparent.
Palette	A place to mix and hold colors; also, a range of colors.
Perspective Drawing	The technique of reproducing the appearance of reality on a flat plane.

PHOTOSHOP
The native 24-bit file format of Photoshop. Once a file is opened in Photoshop, it can be changed from RGB (screen colors) to CMYK (process colors) which is necessary for process printing.

PICT
A commonly used Macintosh format for both object-oriented and bit-mapped graphics files.

Pixel
Picture element; the smallest element that can be manipulated to form letters, numbers, or graphics.

Pointillism
A method of drawing or painting a series of small dots to create a piece of artwork.

Portrait
An art form that represents human or animal faces.

PostScript
A page description language that offers flexible font capability and high-quality graphics.

Pressure-Sensitive Tablet
An electronic drawing pad used with a pointing device (stylus).

Primary Colors
The basis for mixing all other colors red, blue and yellow.

Process Color
A method of handling color by which each block of color is separated into cyan, magenta, yellow, and black (the color components necessary for printing).

RAM
Random access memory; computer allocation for the temporary storage of information.

Raster Graphics
A method of creating graphics where images are stored as pixels arranged in rows and columns.

Resolution
The measurement of the clarity or detail presented by a monitor or printer in producing an image.

RGB   Red, Green, Blue; the three basic components of light combined to create a color image on the monitor.

RIFF   Raster Image File Format; the file format used for raster graphics.

Saturation   Part of the HSB (Hue-Saturation-Brightness) color model; saturation is the amount of a hue contained in a color (the greater the saturation, the more intense the color).

Scan   A digitized image of text, photo or graphics.

Secondary Color   The result of mixing of two primary colors.

Seurat   Artist who pioneered the pointillism style of art.

Shade   A color with black added to it.

Shadow   The dark reflection of an image cast by an object intercepting light.

Shapes   Spatial objects created with connected and closed lines.

Silhouette   The two-dimensional representation of the outline of an object, as a cutout or outline drawing, filled with a solid color (usually black).

Spot Color   A method of handling color in which a particular color of ink is specified for different areas on a page.

Stencil   The outline of a shape or object that can be filled or used as a mask.

Stippling   A drawing style that uses small, short dots or strokes to produce an image.

Stylus	A pointing device (pen) that is used with a pressure-sensitive tablet.
Symmetrical	The balanced proportion of forms on opposite sides of the center vertical axis in an image.
Targa	A file format, used by high-end PC-based computers, that allows individual selection of resolution for files.
Three-dimensional	The representation of depth, width, and height in an image.
TIFF	Tagged Image File Format; a widely supported graphics file format used to exchange documents between applications.
Tint	A color with white added to it.
Tone	A color with gray added to it.
Transparent	The quality of transmitted visibility through an object or image.
Typeface	The named design set of printed characters, such as Helvetica or Times.
Typography	The artistic process of designing with type.
Value	The quality of lightness or darkness in a color.

INDEX

■ ■ ■ ■ ■ ■ ■ ■ ■ ■ ■ ■

■ ▪ ░ ▪ ■ ▪ ░ ▪ ■ ▪ ░ ▪ ■